LEADERSHIP SKILLS PATHWAY

Managing in the Spirit

A Faith-based Leadership Training Guide
For Church Leaders, Faith-based
Non-profit organizations, Team Leaders
And Anyone In A Leadership Role

PASTOR JIM OLAIZ, JR.

Leadership Skills Pathway: Managing in the Spirit

Published 2025
Printed in the United States of America
First Edition

ISBN (softcover): 978-1-967482-96-4
ISBN (e-book): 978-1-967482-97-1

Holzer Books LLC
8 The Green, Ste. A
Dover, Delaware 19901 USA

For information about special discounts available for bulk purchases, sales promotions, and educational needs, contact:

info@holzerbooksllc.com
+1 (888) 901-7776

holzerbooksLLC©

DEDICATION AND ACKNOWLEDGEMENTS

DEDICATED TO MY LORD

First and foremost, I want to thank and praise my Lord and Savior Jesus Christ. He is truly the author and finisher of my faith as well as this guidebook. It is through the power of the Holy Spirit that I hope that the information contained within these pages will inspire, educate and raise the commitment of service of the church body of Christ to bring glory to Him.

ACKNOWLEDGEMENTS
MY WIFE

I cannot express enough thanks and gratitude to my wife Lucy for all her love and support throughout my ministry service and the development of this guidebook. It has been because of her patience and understanding of the time I took to develop this material, when I could have spent more time with her, that I truly appreciate.

To you, my deepest gratitude. Your encouragement when the times got rough have been much appreciated and duly noted. It was a great comfort and relief to know that you were willing to take extra care of our household while I completed my work.
Thank you, my love!

MY FAMILY AND FRIENDS

To each and every one of my sons, their families; and friends, for their love and joy in my life.

MY PARTNERS AND SUPPORTERS

To my friends, encouragers and financial supporters- Pastor Greg N., Ross S., Jose S., Manny DLH, Mario R., Jan G., Pastor Jim S., Gary R. and Sharon R., whose continued encouragement, like Barnabas was to the apostle Paul, throughout these past few years to press on and complete the work that the Lord had started in me, through the enabling of the Holy Spirit into my mind and hands. Thank you, all!

To my childhood friend Mark Johnson, whom I've always regarded as a brother. It was your professional editing of this material that brought polish and professionalism to the work God planned for all that read this guidebook. Many will yield great blessings because of your commitment to the work done by you. Thank you, Mark!

**My completion of this project could not have been accomplished without my God-given abilities and the support of everyone mentioned
Thank you!**

ABSTRACT

Managing in the Spirit

Ministry management is woven with a two-fold fabric- a spiritual fiber and a practical fiber. The spiritual fiber speaks about a person's heart for God. His or her calling may manifest itself as a subtle voice or can be as obvious as reading an illuminated billboard driving along the highway. In any case, without Jesus instilling and then developing a desire to serve, we work in the flesh. In other words, a person called is a person led.

Each one of Jesus' apostles was personally called out. None of them campaigned or designated themselves to the responsibility that changed their lives forever. Each responded to a personal invitation from our Lord. Their ministry training was both intensely spiritual and practical, which grew exponentially to their last day of service.

The practical fiber is the administrative application of ministry management. Those called to ministry service must prepare themselves to manage the day-to-day activities, which serve as the infrastructure for leadership. Selecting men and women of sound counsel, designing an arterial flow of the various ministries, keeping the books, training those who will train and develop others, delegating duties to broaden a proper responsive scope are all examples of practical leadership.

Moreover, when a pastor, staff member, elder, deacon or leader in a secular role responds to a calling from the Lord and develops their administrative gift, these activities are no longer burdensome. Conversely, their personal gift becomes a leadership gift to the Body of Christ. We have been provided with a valuable lesson in this regard. In Acts 6:3 church leadership responded to a need by demonstrating their; leadership, delegation and conflict management skills to name a few- "Therefore brethren, select from among you seven men of good reputation, full of the Spirit and of wisdom, whom we may put in charge of this task."

The goal of this manual is to prepare ministry servants and enhance their God-given gifts as they serve the Body of Christ and the greater good. The question now before you is- *Are you ready to grow in the calling that the Lord has placed in your life? If so, let's get started!*

LEARNING OBJECTIVES

Leadership Skills Pathway: Managing in the Spirit

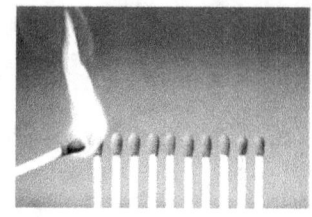

MODULE LEARNING OBJECTIVES:

- **The Gift of Administration:** Examine yourself and unearth your gift of administration through your existing personality traits and attributes.

  > "And God has appointed in the church, first apostles, second prophets, third teachers, then miracles, then gifts of healings, helps, administrations, various kinds of tongues."
  > I Corinthians 12:28

- **Planning:** Learn to define a goal and provide direction for completing it.

  > "For which one of you, when he wants to build a tower, does not first sit down and calculate the cost to see if he has enough to complete it?" Luke 14:28-30

- **Organization:** Learn to develop structure for a plan, which will best utilize people and resources to accomplish a goal.

  > "A plan in the heart of a man is like deep water, but a man of understanding draws it out." Proverbs 20:5

- **Delegation:** Expand your scope of responsibility by utilizing and developing others to accomplish a goal.

  > ". . . So the twelve summoned the congregation of the disciples and said, "It is not desirable for us to neglect the word of God in order to serve tables. But select from among you, brethren, seven men of good reputation, full of the Spirit and of wisdom, whom we may put in charge of this task." Acts 6:1-6

- **Communication:** Discover the process we go through to convey thoughts and actions from one person or group to another.

> "The Lord said, Behold, they are one people, and they all
> have the same language. And this is what they began to do,
> and now nothing which they purpose to do will be
> impossible for them." Genesis 11:6

- **Problem Solving:** Learn to generate solutions that work, instead of putting out fires that reignite.

> "So give your servant an understanding heart to judge your
> people to discern between good and evil." I Kings 3:9

- **Decision-Making:** Understand the basic principles of selecting the best course of action.

> ". . . The King said, "Divide the living child in two, and give
> half to the one and half to the other." I Kings 3: 16-28

- **Time Management:** Explore principles that will bring order to your time and activities, which can optimize your efforts.

> "Therefore be careful how you walk, not as unwise men, but
> as wise, making the most of your time, because the days are
> evil." Ephesians 5:15-16

- **Conflict Management:** Develop skills which will empower you to mediate issues small or great.

> "Blessed are the peacemakers, for they shall be called sons
> of God." Matthew 5:9

- **Servant-Leadership:** Learn God's definition of leadership as you improve your servant's heart.

". . . shepherd the flock of God among you, exercising oversight not under compulsion, but voluntarily, according to the will of God; and not for sordid gain, but with eagerness; nor yet as lording it over those allotted to your charge, but proving to be examples to the flock."
I Peter 5:2-3

- **Ministry Financial Stewardship:** Sharpen your knowledge of managing by leveraging a ministry's or an organization's resources for God's work.

    "In this case, moreover, it is required of stewards that one be found trustworthy." I Corinthians 4:2

- **Ministry Organizational Development:** Identifying and understanding the key concepts of Organizational Development (OD); as it relates to theory, and practice dedicated to expanding the knowledge and effectiveness of people to accomplish more successful organizational change and performance.

    "The mind of a man plans his way, But the Lord directs his path." Proverbs 16:19

- **Vison and Mission Development:** Acquire a comprehension of the underpinning of any organization. Through this module, expect to gain insights which powerfully explain how an organization can effectively communicate the purpose, values and future of an organization.

    "Then the Lord answered me and said, "Record the vision and inscribe it on tablets, That the one who reads it may run. "For the vision is yet for the appointed time; It hastens toward the goal, and it will not fail. Though it tarries, wait for it; For it will certainly come, it will not delay."
    Habakkuk 2:2-3

SUMMARY:

We know that the goal of every believer should be to share the gospel with the world at large. Our Lord affirmed this when He said:

> **"Do you not say, "There are yet four months, and then comes the harvest?" Behold, I say to you, lift up your eyes and look on the fields, that they are white for harvest." John 4:35**

Knowing this, the goal of these modules is to provide a comprehensive training curriculum which will equip all those who are called to service. The Lord spent many hours teaching His apostles the attributes needed to fulfill His great "commission". In that same vein, for those who are called, your commitment must be strategic, deliberate, and focused. Allow these modules are intended to be stepping-stones in your journey of service.

Furthermore, as you develop, you will find that there are myriads of resources to enhance and strengthen your learning experience. Then, as the Lord leads you, learn to collect these precious gems of knowledge and utilize them for the benefit of the Body of Christ.

Table of Contents

The Gift of Administration

How others assess your work, the joy, or interest you have in managerial activity and the Holy Spirit's witness in your life are indicators of the gift of Administration – Ken Gangel[1]

Hat is the gift of Administration? Peter reveals to us that every Christian is given at least one "special" gift to be used for the service of one another by the grace of God (I Peter 4:10). It is in the Apostle Paul's list of personal gifts where we find the gift of Administration.

> **And God has appointed in the church, first apostles, second prophets, third teachers, then miracles, then gifts of healings, helps, Administrations, various kinds of tongues. (I Corinthians 12:28).**

I Corinthians 12:4-5 states that there are varieties of "gifts" or "charismas", as in spiritual endowment, and varieties of "ministries", or "diakonia", from the root meaning for attendant, servant or as in an official capacity or service, e.g., minister, teacher, deacon, servant, etc. Although these two words are distinct from each other, they work in unison to serve the Body of Christ.

The actual gift of Administration or practical "diakonia" that is referred to in I Corinthians 12:28 refers to an "office or function". The Greek word for "Administrations" found in I Corinthians 12:28 literally translated is "kubernesis" from the word "kubernao", meaning to steer, pilot, or helmsman, i.e., directorship (in the church). This speaks to a position or office which someone either is appointed to or pursues on their own.

Typically, a leader who possesses the gift of Administration may also be gifted with a <u>charismatic</u> gift or gifts which serve as a companion to their gift of Administration. The addition of a "charisma" gifting works to enhance a leader's administrative role.

Administration, as an office, can be developed. For example, activities like planning, organizing, delegating, or time management help to improve skill sets that are needed. This aspect of the gift of Administration allows for the individual to constantly work at improving his/her gifting and eventually coach or train others who may be gifted in this same capacity.

A significant characteristic of the gift of Administration is that it conveys authority. This authority may come in a variety of ways, such as:

- In business you may be promoted or appointed

- In politics you may be elected or succeed an incumbent

- In ministry you may be called or appointed

In each case, all of these examples are visible, definable, objective and tangible.

As stated earlier, the charismatic side of administration or personal abilities ("charisma") serves to enhance the gift of Administration. These gifts are a specific spiritual endowments given to a believer which, as a leader, can be exercised in the role of an administrator. These gifts are special to each recipient and come from the Holy Spirit. The "charisma" gifts that are listed in Romans 12:6-8; I Corinthians 12:4-11 are as follows- (pay particular attention to the "leads" gift)

- Prophecy – speak under divine inspiration

- Service – to minister or serve

- Teaches – to instruct

- Exhorts – to encourage and edify others

- Gives – to share

- Mercy – to have compassion or pity

- Leads (Romans 12:8) – Greek word is "proistemi". Meaning, to stand before (as in rank) to rule, to be over, preside over, etc. This "charismatic" gift speaks of a spiritual endowment which a leader exercises in his or her role of administration.

The characteristics of these charismatic gifts are transparent, emotional, and inspirational, and can dynamically enhance the work of administration. Some examples of these types of gifts can be seen in these statements-

- "I don't know what it is, but he's got it."

- "She's kept this place running for 30 years."

- "Even though he's third string, he's an inspiration to all of us."

The key is to utilize the charismatic gifts to optimize the gift of Administration!

The personal gift (charismatic) and the administration (kubernesis) gift ought not to be confused. The gift of Administration or "diakonia" functions as a sovereign grant by the Holy Spirit and is typically meant for administrating the work of the Church or some specific kingdom-ministry. In contrast, the skill of being able to lead and organize an endeavor may be a natural or innate talent that some people possess, but this does not mean that they are necessarily called by God to lead administratively over a ministry.

In Romans 12:8, Paul emphasizes a very active approach to manifesting this gift of Administration- ". . . he who leads with <u>diligence</u>." This active role may be exercised in a variety of ways. However, the material covered in these modules will focus on the gift's relevance to a person's ministry calling through practical application.

Two-Fold Characteristic

Ministry management is woven with a two-fold fabric:

- A spiritual fiber (charismatic) which;

- Speaks of a heart for God

- Without the Lord instilling and then developing a desire to serve, we work in the flesh

- A person that is called, is a person led by the Spirit

- A practical fiber (practical) which;

- Is the administrative application of ministry management

- Ministers to the needs of the day-to-day activities which builds up the infrastructure of the church or ministry

- Appoints men and women to keep the arterial flow of the church going by serving in capacities like, keeping the books, training others, cleaning the church, serving as ushers, etc.

- When a Pastor, Elder, Deacon, ministry leader, faith-based or faith-centered leader develops their administrative gift, their service activities help to relieve any issues of burden

- Becomes a ministry gift to the Body of Christ

By weaving both fabrics, a complete implementation of the administrative gifting becomes a powerful and effective gift for the Body of Christ. This balance is necessary to avoid either omitting God from the picture or causing confusion by ignoring strategic direction.

The question, which you may be thinking at this point is- "How do I know if I possess the personal gift of Administration?" There is no test to pass or magic formula which reveals whether the gift of Administration abides within you. However, you can rely on several factors which can help you distinguish if you possess this gift.

First, the Holy Spirit does lead and speak to us (John 15:26, Romans 8:14, II Peter 1:21). Any believer who is in tune with God's calling may begin the process with an idea, a feeling, a thought, or a recurring scripture verse. As a word of caution, however, be careful that at the end of your search and confirmation of your gift, that you are not the only one with this revelation. Any gift we possess will either be validated by others or will be evident in the demonstration of the gift in our everyday walk.

Second, self-appointment is not necessarily a confirmation. In other words, others may serve as a witness to your gift and may call you to serve and utilize your gift. Your true calling will also underscore your gift for the service in ministry.

Third, mirror your strengths and weakness against those examples of godly leaders in the Scriptures. Several administrator models can be found throughout the pages of God's word. Compare yourself to these models and ask yourself, "How closely do I emulate their examples?"

Finally, with a few exceptions, there should be a resounding "Amen" in your heart confirming your gift. Like Moses or Paul, some have been pulled into service, but ordinarily you will know God's calling and your gift of Administration in your leadership role.

Leaders with the personal gift of Administration will provide leadership in running a smooth and well-organized ministry. Their gift will be manifested in their ability for, example to, plan, organize, communicate, and solve problems or team-build with other leaders in their ministry.

One serious challenge may arise if a person with the gift of Administration fails to recognize that not everyone possesses the same gifting. This oversight may lead to frustration and a reoccurring tendency of doing everything themselves. Others may fail to do it as they would do it or with the same veracity. As a precaution to this challenge, work on developing your delegating skills and learn to accept that at times a task or project may be done in a different manner.

CAN A GIFT BE DEVELOPED?

In Ephesians 4:12, the apostle Paul speaks of "equipping" a believer in Christ for the benefit of the Body of Christ. In Hebrews 13:21 we see the author referring to being equipped by Jesus Christ to do work which is pleasing in His sight. Clearly, we see an endowment from Christ. But, what about cases where someone is asked or appointed to serve? Can the Gift of Administration be developed to fulfill a need or function?

We see this type of appointment in the book of Acts, chapter thirteen. The Holy Spirit gave the instruction to separate Barnabas and Paul for a specific service or function. In responding to this appointment, they were enabled or equipped to complete their task at hand.

In Acts 6, we see another illustration of someone being selected for service. The apostles called the congregation together to appoint seven men to attend to the needs of the ministry. Again, their appointment was premised on their visible gifts, which made them viable candidates.

 The point of this section is to simply convey that if you have never identified the gift of Administration in your life, do not worry. The administrative skills and talents needed to lead a ministry can be developed. In fact, you may be developing these needed skills in your current occupation and not even realizing it. Therefore, making the transition from your secular role to your ministry calling may be simpler than expected.

GIFT OF ADMINISTRATION PROFILE

Simply put, a balanced Christian church, faith-based or faith-centered organization needs two forms of administration, practical and spiritual. These are split into two bodies primarily to prevent the pastor, elders or Christian leaders from being distracted by secular matters. The key to achieving balance is to accurately identify the gifting that each leader possesses and utilize those leaders in their proper roles according to their gifting. Below is a profile of the gift of Administration:

Role: The ability to provide direction for the goals of the Church, ministry or organization by designing and executing an efficient plan of action. This includes a strong understanding of how all people can best be utilized to meet these goals.

Meaning: *To pilot/steer a ship.* This role is fulfilled by someone who actually gets the Church, a ministry or an organization where it wants to go by God's leading.

Key traits: Vision-minded, thorough, objective, responsible, organized, detail-oriented, efficient, conscientious, to name a few.

Characteristics: *This is a person who can…*

- Develop strategies or plans to reach identified goals

- Assist staff, volunteers or ministries to become more effective and efficient

- Create order out of organizational chaos

- Manage or coordinate a variety of responsibilities to accomplish a task

- Organize people, tasks, or events … *and enjoys doing it.*

Precautions/Liabilities:

- May rely on their well-organized plans rather than the Spirit and prayer

- May be too careful and block the overall vision with their many specific details

- May be unresponsive to suggestions and changes in plans from others

- Could use people simply to accomplish goals without being concerned for their growth in the process.

Scripture: 1 Corinthians 2:28, Acts 6:1-7; Exodus. 18:13-26

Example: Joseph, Moses, Nehemiah, Solomon

The following section may be used as a tool to help you in discovering whether you possess the gift of Administration or the charismatic gift of leading. There are no right or wrong answers It's only function is to stimulate thoughts and aid you in reflecting on your calling.

CHARACTER QUALITIES AND PERSONAL TRAITS OF THOSE POSSSESSING THE PERSONAL GIFT OF ADMINISTRATION[2]

Review the following character qualities and personality traits. Highlight those that apply to you and spend some time reflecting on each one.

1.   Possess an ability to integrate several ministries, people tasks, and/or projects towards the fulfillment of long-range goal.

2.   Is sensitive to future needs, particular to future needs that are not being planned for by others.

3.   Has an ability to visualize overall needs and to clarify long-range goals.

4.   Has an ability to assist an individual by designing and setting up a ministry or an area of responsibility that offers that individual the greatest personal satisfaction because it makes the fullest use of the individual's talents, resources, and gifts.

5.   Has an ability to put together individuals to form efficient, well-organized teams-teams on which the members work well together, divide their labor efficiently, and enjoy each other's company.

6.   Has an ability to discuss the talents, resources, and spiritual gifts of individuals.

7.   Has ability to discern and unify available resources toward the fulfillment of a goal.

8.   Tends to assume responsibility if no structured leadership exits.

9.   Desires to see that his time and the time of others are used efficiently.

10. Tends to insist on thorough planning and organization before embarking on a new task or new ministry.

11. Tends to avoid the develop-as-you-go type of ministries, projects or initiatives. He/She wants things done right from the beginning.

12. Demonstrates a willingness to wait on a project or ministry until it is properly set up. Once a project or ministry is set up, however; he/she will push for maximum speed in accomplishing its goals.

13. Is strongly motivated to organize anything for which he/she is responsible.

14. Has an ability to make use of the resources available now, not waiting for future resources to develop.

15. Is motivated to delegate, if possible.

16. Has an ability to know what can or cannot be delegated.

17. Is sensitive to recognize and to acknowledge other people's hidden achievements that have helped in reaching a goal.

18. Tends to put high priority on loyalty in selecting people for a team.

19. Tends to be neat and orderly in everything: home, appearance, job, other activities (even recreation), and projects.

20. Is reluctant to pay for organizational services, preferring to perform this him/herself. He/She prefers to make proposals rather than ask for bids. He/She wants to be his/her own contractor.

21. Tends to assign tasks or solve problems with his eyes on the future impact of his decisions and actions.

22. Is able and willing to endure reaction from others in order to accomplish an ultimate goal in a minimum amount of time. He/She recognizes that others are not as sensitive as he/she may be to the overall picture or the importance of the goal.

23. Is strongly motivated to help others become more efficient in carrying out tasks.

24. Recognizes the importance of maintaining good records and of writing clear instructions. He/She sees that with these aids a task can be easily repeated in the future or in some different context.

25. Places a high premium on reliability and responsibility.

26. Tends to avoid the limelight. However, he/she definitely enjoys the role of a strategic commander working behind the scenes.

27. Tends to remain firm and steadfast, regardless of opposition, once he/she has determined that a particular goal is in God's will.

28. Believes strongly in the importance of keeping commitments even in adverse or difficult circumstances.

29. Appreciates initiative. He/She values people who can foresee problems and take action to prevent or correct them without having to get detailed instructions.

30. Demonstrates an ability to finalize difficult decisions, though he/she is very careful and deliberate to first examine all of the pertinent facts.

31. May appear to be a perfectionist because he/she insists on detailed planning and preparation.

32. May tend to overlook spiritual weaknesses and faults of key persons on the teams that he/she designs because he/she focuses almost solely on the personal talents, training, and spiritual gifts that will be useful for achieving a particular goal.

33. If problems exist in his/her organization, tends to handle them by readjusting the responsibilities and positions of individuals on the team in order to achieve more compatible working relationships (as opposed to first solving individuals' personal problems).

34. Is strongly motivated to look for and move on to a new challenge whenever a project comes to completion. If this motivation is highly exercised, he/she may get the reputation of being an empire builder.

35. Receives great fulfillment in seeing all the pieces of a project fitting together and in seeing others enjoying the finished product.

SUMMARY

Obviously, not everyone who is in leadership will possess the gift of Administration. Some will possess other valuable gifts that enable them to fulfill their calling. Never the less, it is important to recognize the components necessary in managing any ministry: planning, organizing, delegating, communicating, etc., are essential in achieving God's plan for leadership.

Just as someone who is called and gifted to teach can hone their skills at communication and become a more effective communicator over time and experience, so the person who is called to lead and given the gift of Administration can develop their skills. This is what Peter means when he says we must be good stewards with the manifold grace of God (I Peter 4:10). Even as the servants in the parable were allotted different amounts of talents and told to invest them, it was only the two who actually put their gifts to work that were commended. The one servant who failed to use his gift and develop it into something more was rebuked, and ultimately lost his place as a servant in the household.

As you work through in developing the managerial skills necessary to effectively and efficiently shepherd a ministry, do not overlook your <u>attitude</u>. Clearly, our attitude should be in line with what Paul described to us in Philippians 2:5-7. Here it speaks of Jesus' humility in serving the world around Him. He laid aside His mighty power and glory to take on the guise of a bondservant. He led by serving.

Myron Rush, president of a Colorado based consulting firm, who works with both secular and Christian organizations, shared some words of wisdom from a Christian leader he knew. He was quoted to say, "I have discovered that if you *train* a man, he will become what you are, but, if you *serve* him, the sky is the limit as to what he can become"[3]. These are powerful words.

References

1. Kenn Gangel, *Coaching Ministry Teams*, (Nashville, TN: Thomas Nelson, Inc., 2000), pages 21.

2. Ted W. Engstrom, *Your Gift of Administration, How to Discover and Use It*, (Nashville, TN: Thomas Nelson, Inc., 1983), pages 30-34.

3. Myron Rush, *Management: A Biblical Approach*, (Wheaton, IL: Victor Books, 1985), pages 13-14.

PERSONAL APPLICATION

1. Review the list of 35 traits of administrators and list, which align with your abilities and desires. Explain, generally, why you think so. Give some examples.

2. Prayerfully, seek to confirm if you possess the gift of Administration. There are no time restrictions or timeframe in which to do this. It may reveal itself very quickly or it may take time to discern if you possess the gift at all.

3. On two separate sheets of paper write the secular definition of "Management is getting work done through others" and the biblical definition of "Management is meeting the needs of others as they work at accomplishing their tasks or jobs". Ask various people you work with to describe what each definition of management communicates to them and what they perceive their management thinks of them as employees.

4. Make a list of your strengths and weaknesses as a leader or manager. As you go through this exercise, list the principles and tools you need to improve your leadership and/or administrative skills.

Planning

By wisdom a house is built, and by understanding it is established: And by knowledge the rooms are filled with all precious and pleasant riches. Proverbs 24:3-4

The wisdom spoken in Proverbs 24:3-4 implies wise planning. Moreover, the house can represent an individual, a family, a ministry or an organization. Implementing preplanned actions reduces the impact of the unforeseen and minimizes the exhaustive effort that goes into putting out "fires" that arise unexpectedly.

"Purposes and goals point direction. Priorities help us to choose which goals are most important. Planning is the *stuff* that converts goals into action and dreams into reality." [1]

Strategic and effective planning tangibly demonstrates the direction of ideas and visions. The planning process states the purpose or goal. Supported by sub-levels of objectives that under-gird the actions needed to successfully complete the goal.

"For which one of you, when he wants to build a tower, does not first sit down and calculate the cost to see if he has enough to complete it?" Luke 14:28

The word "calculate" in this context is a mathematical term, which literally means to count pebbles or to compute. This is an action which talks about deliberately assessing the- who, what, where, why, when, and how something is to be done. Conversely, the omission of any one of these elements weakens the success of accomplishing the intended goal.

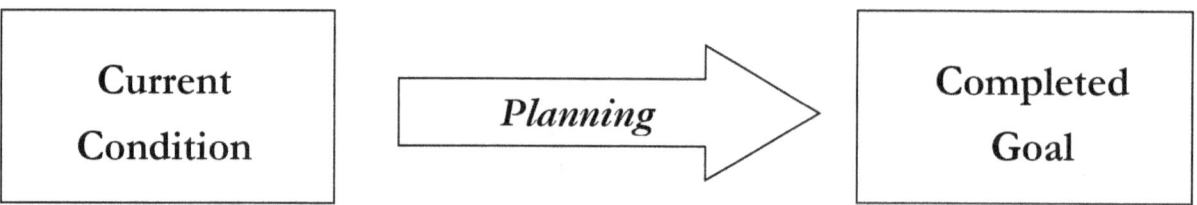

The preceding graphic illustration depicts planning in its simplest form. "Things as they are" is the "Current condition". "Things as we want them to be" is the "Completed Goal" which is desired. Planning is the conduit that moves you from point A to point B. It's important to note that planning is a living and growing process. When a plan becomes fixed or inflexible, the likelihood of failure increases.

Planning by definition is identifying the purpose of a project or process, defining the activities to be performed, their sequence and the resources needed to accomplish the goal.

> *"For I know the plans I have for you, declares the Lord, plans for*
> *welfare and not for calamity to give you a future and a hope."*
> *Jeremiah 29:11*

The Lord here had Jeremiah's future in mind, and He has the same for everyone who takes the time to listen to His calling. Often in scripture, we see that the Lord instructs us in the way we should go. What we, as followers of Christ, should understand emphatically is that we must seek God's guidance in all our planning. When we step out in our own power rather than God's, we gamble on the outcome and risk accomplishing something that may not have been intended by Him, sometimes to our detriment.

WHY SHOULD CHRISTIANS PLAN?

Christians should plan because we should lead orderly lives.

"For God is not a God of confusion but of peace." I Corinthians 14:33.

If God's activities are not characterized by confusion, then neither should the activities of the Christian be characterized in this manner. The apostle Paul reinforces the principle when he states,

"But let all things be done properly in an orderly manner."
I Corinthians 14:40

Also, since we are to be imitators of Jesus (Ephesians 5:1), we must then strive to minimize confusion in our lives.

Have you ever gone all the way to the store and returned only to discover that you forgot something on your list or missed an errand on the way? This can happen in your workplace or other areas of responsibility as well. For example, without a plan, you can forget to book a speaker for a conference until it is too late, or get started on one activity only to find out that you should have completed a higher priority task first.

Christians should plan because Christ advocates thinking ahead. Previously, Luke 14:28 was quoted, but if you read on, it explains why we need to plan. Reading through to verse thirty-two, we see that actions without planning lead to ridicule and failure. Therefore, through careful planning we can understand what the eventual commitment or sacrifice will entail.

Furthermore, Christians should plan because we need to be moving toward goals, not just fighting fires (constantly trying to solve one urgent problem after another).

Have you ever said, "I didn't get anything done today?" You must have spent your time doing something? However, you probably did not accomplish anything that seemed "productive". Very likely, urgent or unforeseen things interrupted you all day. It is a natural tendency to react to urgent matters that press you to respond. Yet, some of these things may not have been a high priority.

A valuable key to planning is developing discernment for what really is a priority. Learning to either say "No" or at least negotiate when or how you can respond to a request can lead to a better use of your time and resources.

Remember:

> *"The mind of man plans his way, But the Lord directs his steps."*
> *Proverbs 16:9*

ELEMENTS OF PLANNING

• PRAYER

Everything starts and ends with prayer. God's wisdom for any plan is imperative for the success. If the plan is not what God intended, you risk wasting time and resources.

It is important to note that we need to be sensitive and open-mined to His leading. Sometimes the Lord leads us in very unconventional methods and approaches. Imagine Joshua's thoughts when the Lord outlined the plan for taking Jericho (Joshua 6:2-5).

The Lord is clearly the power behind anything we attempt. God has a plan for all His people. When we recognize that the first step in any plan is to seek His counsel, we ensure we are headed in the right direction. We must realize, as believers in Jesus, our responsibility is to seek the Lord's will and then "trust" God for the results.

> *"Many are the plans in a man's heart, but it is the Lord's plan that prevails" Proverbs 19:21 (NIV)*

- **ESTABLISH THE OVERALL PURPOSE OF THE PROJECT**

<u>Identifying the purpose is essential in setting the course of the project.</u> Every journey begins with a first step. Planning is no different. That first step is knowing the purpose of the journey or project. Some of the questions that may arise and should be answered are:

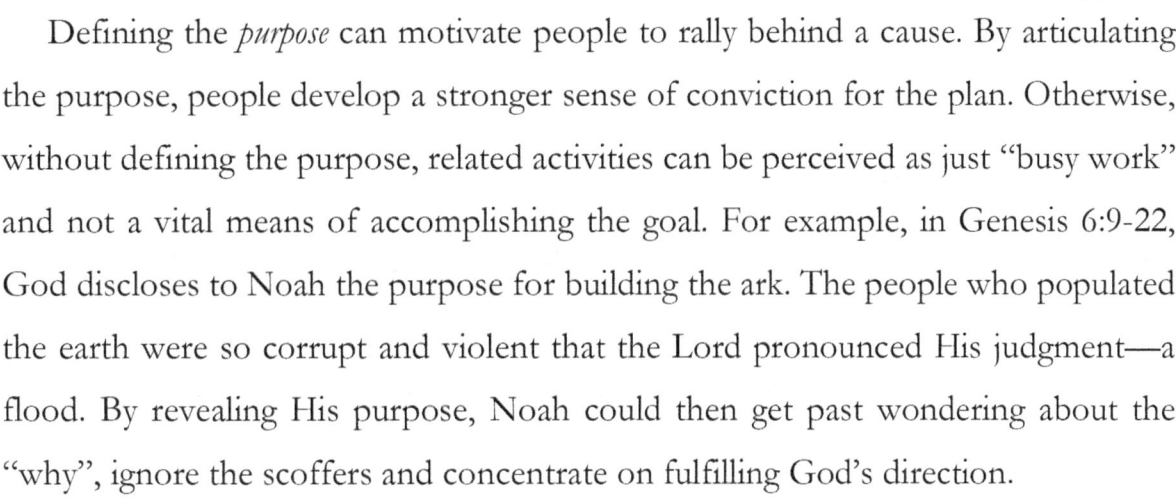

1. Why is this project or task important?
2. Why do we need to invest in this?
3. Why should this be a priority?
4. Do we need to do this now?
5. How will it enhance our present condition?
6. Is this of the Lord?

Defining the *purpose* can motivate people to rally behind a cause. By articulating the purpose, people develop a stronger sense of conviction for the plan. Otherwise, without defining the purpose, related activities can be perceived as just "busy work" and not a vital means of accomplishing the goal. For example, in Genesis 6:9-22, God discloses to Noah the purpose for building the ark. The people who populated the earth were so corrupt and violent that the Lord pronounced His judgment—a flood. By revealing His purpose, Noah could then get past wondering about the "why", ignore the scoffers and concentrate on fulfilling God's direction.

The pitfall of many organizers is to move right into how the goal will be achieved and overlook the necessity of explaining the purpose. Unless the purpose is clearly understood, the project or activity can be become just an exercise in tradition or mindless routine.

One benefit of identifying the purpose early is that you confirm buy-in before you begin the process of "what" needs to be accomplished. Then sequentially, goals and objectives can be set, which in turn enable you and your co-laborers to envision the finished product.

Another benefit is that the "buy-in" people will develop critical thinking skills and you can utilize them as they progress through the project. For example, you cannot adequately determine how much money will be spent or how to sequence activities unless you understand why you are moving in a certain direction. Imagine handing building blueprints to people within a church ministry and asking them to just follow the prints without question. Mid-way some may realize they are building a church, but by then, an enormous amount of creative and critical thinking may be lost. As a result, valuable time and/or resources are squandered unnecessarily.

Unfortunately, for many people, planning is merely filling out a budget form or creating an annual calendar, without giving it much thought. But by disclosing the purpose, a leader can remove any obstacles which can stifle creative and critical thinking.

• DEVELOP GOALS AND OBJECTIVES

Goals and Objectives 101: Questions & Answers:

What is a Goal?

- The final purpose or aim. The end to which a plan is completed; or which a person aims to attain.

What is an Objective?

- An activity or action that works toward achieving a goal. The "how" of a goal.

Which comes first, the goal or the objective?

- The goal is established first, followed by the supporting objectives that will provide the means to successfully reach the goal.

How do you measure them?

- Establish milestones or checkpoints to monitor the progress. Dates, quotas, identifiable completed tasks, all serve as measurements of completion.

Why do I want to measure objectives?

- Primarily the purpose of measuring objectives is to confirm that you are on track in reaching a goal. Without any measuring standards, valuable resources such as money, staff and time will be wasted. Lack of measuring objectives may demonstrate poor stewardship of God's provisions.

How do I determine the sequence of objectives?

- As you begin discussions, establish what the single result of your goal should be. Then identify what activities are necessary to complete the goal. Once you have identified all the activities, step back and analyze the logical sequence of events. Some activities will stand out and some will need to be discussed at length. However, be flexible to adjust your sequence as needed.

How do I delegate who does what?

- Once the major areas of activities are identified, begin matching people's natural talents and abilities to fit the task(s). The most important factor in selecting someone to take responsibility and ownership of a task or activity is the desire to do it. All the talents and abilities in a person will not help them in following through with a responsibility if their heart is not in it. Make sure that you ask for a statement of commitment from the person you select. Do not pressure them, just because you think they are a good fit. Share with them about the time and commitment required and let them decide if the fit is right.

The Goal Development Process:

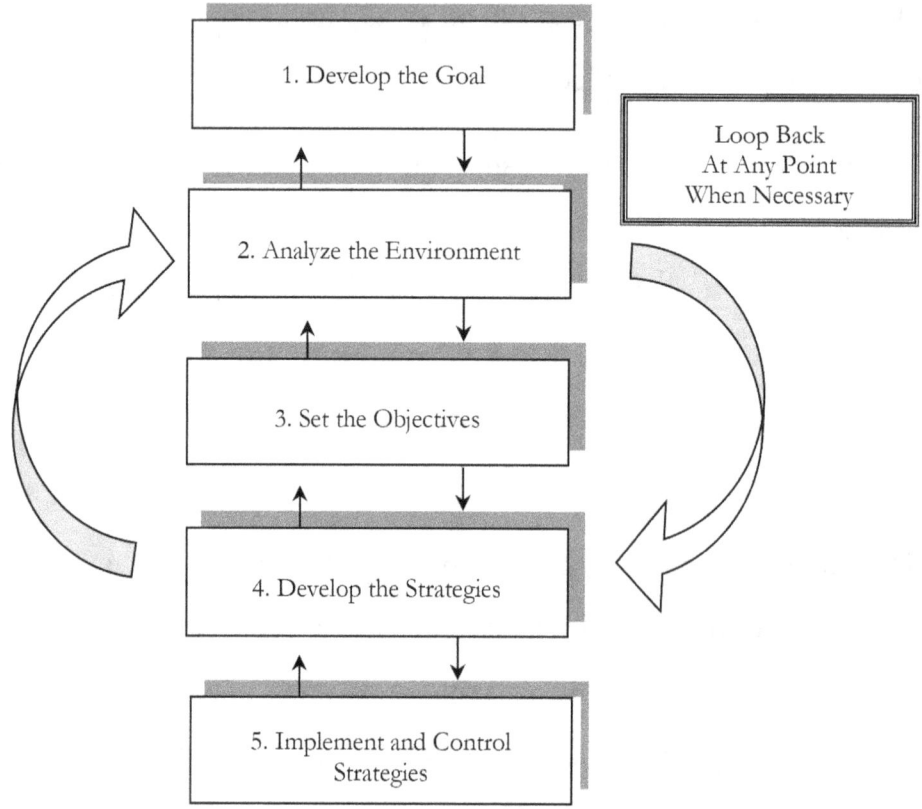

CRITERIA FOR GOALS OR OBJECTIVES USING THE "S.M.A.R.T. GOAL" FORMAT

Singular Result: Goal or Objective Preface

To avoid confusion, each goal or objective should contain only *one* result. If multiple results are listed, one may be met, but the other(s) may not be.

Specific:

A well-defined goal must be **specific**. A goal or objective is specific if it can be clearly stated in one to two sentences, but no more than a short paragraph. Longer stated goals that are more complex replace clarity with confusion and shift the goal's focus from quality to quantity.

A specific goal has a much greater chance of being accomplished than a general goal.

To set a specific goal you must answer the six "W" questions:

- Who: Who is involved?

- What: What do I want to accomplish?

- Where: Identify a location

- When: Establish a time frame

- Which: Identify requirements and constraints

- Why: Specific reason, purpose or benefits of
                accomplishing the goal

EXAMPLE: A general goal would be, "Get in shape." But a specific goal would say, "Join a health club and workout 3 days a week."

*M*easurable:

For a goal to be **measurable,** you need a way to measure the progress and some specific criteria that will tell you when you can stop and the goal is achieved. Seeing the progress is very important for you to stay motivated and enjoy the process of achieving the goal. The more quantified a goal is, the more likely it will be that the goal is measurable.

*A*ttainable:

A goal is **attainable** when you establish a realistic path to achievement and reasonable odds that you can get there. This does not mean that the lower you aim the more likely you reach success. It is well known that goals work best when they are challenging. Create the goals as ambitious as possible, but still attainable. Then the goal will give you more motivation and a more rewarding sense of achievement.

*R*ewarding:

A goal is **rewarding** when you have clear reasons why you want to reach that goal. This is one more place where it is important that the goal is really worth achieving. Have your specific reasons and expected rewards in writing. If possible, use pictures.

Imagine how you are going to feel when the goal is finally reached. This will ensure that the goal is really worth achieving. Then, whenever you are at an impasse or do not feel motivated, you should reflect back on why you established your goal. This is a very powerful, practical technique for getting through difficult moments without quitting.

*T*ime:

A goal should have a specific **time** limit. Setting up milestones and timelines provides a visual reference as you work through the project. Time is the price you pay for the reward in achieving a goal. Setting a deadline will protect you from paying a higher price than the goal is worth. This is also your protection from procrastination and perfectionism. Deadlines tend to drive an objective to completion of a goal.

Examples of Effective & Ineffective Goals:

A. Ineffective Goal:

Maximize profits in 2008. (How much is "maximized"?)

Effective Goal:

Increase net profits to $1 million in 2008.

B. Ineffective Goal:

Recycle 40% by year end 2008. (40% of what- glass, paper? Type of paper?)

Effective Goal:

Recycle 40% of all paper by year end 2008.

C. Ineffective Goal:

Perfect service for every customer. (How do you measure service?)

Effective Goal:

Attain a 90% customer "excellent" satisfaction rating for 2008

Goal & Objective Hypothetical Examples:

Goal:

- Raise enough money to build a new church building.

Objectives: To have . . .

- A building fund of $500,000.00 by 2016.

- Locate a suitable property for the new building.

- Develop a construction project management plan for the new building.

- Break ground by 2018.

Writing Objectives Model:

Four Parts

1. Infinitive

2. Action verb

3. Singular, specific, measurable and attainable result to be achieved

4. Target date

Example:

(1) To (2) increase (3) the number of trained ministry volunteers from 30 to 40 (4) by June 2010.

The model above is a method for tangibly developing a goal or objective. By breaking down an initial idea and then organizing this thought process, it becomes a constructive and measurable goal or objective.

Now What?

Question?

How do we take our ideas, turn them into goals or objectives, and build upon our foundational building blocks?

Answer:

Assess where you are now. Then, determine the greatest needs of the ministry or organization. Then prioritize them. After you have prioritized them, determine what activities you can do now, and which ones can be done later.

IDENTIFY THE ACTIVITIES AND RESOURCES NECESSARY TO COMPLETE THE PROJECT

After identifying all the activities and resources, set up stepping stones for accomplishing the project. Be open-minded during this process. Encourage the free flow of ideas and suggestions by everyone involved. Afterwards, carve out what is reasonable and realistic.

As a precursor to identifying activities and resources, selecting key people who are willing to accept responsibility is a critical step for the project leader. The selection of these individuals increases a leader's confidence that they can be relied upon to follow through. Two other benefits arise from identifying key people. One, a leader can leverage their expertise to train others during the project or in future projects. Two, as they participate in the planning process their commitment to the project is strengthened.

An important principle to remember is that people have less commitment to the things that they do not own. A simple example is a homeowner versus a renter. Generally, you take great pride in the things you do that enhance your property. Whereas, a renter may do what is minimally required, but may never go beyond that.

Ownership stimulates pride, commitment and motivation. This sense of ownership stimulates participants to be innovative and creative in deciding what activities are necessary to accomplishing a goal.

One tool in identifying activities and resources is collaborative "brainstorming". During brainstorming sessions, ideas and thoughts can be flushed out to begin the planning process. The sole focus of a brainstorming session is to throw out as many ideas and thoughts as possible for consideration. There are no wrong answers, just a multitude of working suggestions which will eventually formulate an operating plan.

Remember to encourage everyone to participate and do not squash anyone's ideas. Always discuss the merits of an idea and determine why it may or may not align with the ultimate goal. Encourage people to improve on traditional methods or ideas and stimulate them to think "out-of-the-box" or out of typical conventions.

ESTABLISH EVENTS AND ACTIVITIES IN A PROPER SEQUENCE

The right activity at the wrong time can be as disastrous as the activity not being performed at all. When the activities are properly sequenced, they describe how the plan will be carried out. It is imperative that the series of events are fully disclosed to avoid confusion among those who have a smaller scope of the project or goal.

Familiarize yourself with the use of a Gantt chart as a tool for sequencing events and activities. A Gantt chart allows you to visually see the course of things as they relate to the project and to each other. As you set up the sequence of things, set milestones or checkpoints to follow-up on the progress of activities. In doing so, you can monitor activities to ensure that things are heading in the right direction and not get off the beaten path.

IDENTIFY THE RESOURCES REQUIRED FOR THE PROJECT

"Or what king, when he sets out to meet another king in battle, will not first sit down and consider whether he is strong enough with ten thousand men to encounter the one coming against him with twenty thousand?" - Luke 14:31

Jesus points out in the verse how valuable it is to sit down and contemplate what we have versus what we need to complete a goal. Time is needed to deliberate in order to avoid being caught short. Without fully considering one's full resources, failure may be immanent.

In Myron Rush's book, "Management: A Biblical Approach"[2], he identifies six factors which are key in allocating resources for a project. He also raises questions that should be considered in the course of planning:

    • People   • Space   • Equipment   • Time   • Money   • Supplies

☑ People

Are you viewing people as the single most important resource? If so, you should consider these questions as you slot people into the activities needed to complete the project:

- What type of skills, gifts and abilities are needed to complete each of the activities?
- Do you currently have people with these skills within the ministry?
- Do you have people interested in developing the skills needed?
- If you go outside the ministry to find the skills, how will you proceed?

☑ Space

What type of space or facilities will be needed? In addition, what is the availability? Facility planning is overlooked far too often in the scheduling portion of a project.

Matching a venue to an event, verifying available dates, securing permits, coordinating people to help set up, etc., are just some examples that need to be considered in planning for space or facilities.

Identifying alternative sites or space should be a part of your contingency planning. Initially the contingency plan can be used to compare costs, but ultimately it can serve as a fallback plan, if needed.

☑ Equipment

What type of equipment is needed and what is the availability? An important point regarding equipment is placing an activity in the proper time sequence. This enables you to know when and how long you will need the equipment.

☑ Supplies

Like equipment, supplies need to be identified in relation to the project and activities. Acquiring and distributing supplies can be time consuming, especially on large projects. Therefore, adequate attention should be given to the type and quantity of supplies to best manage the available resources.

☑ Time

The time necessary to complete various activities will often be a best guess. However, allow time for any events that may not be apparent in the initial planning process. Allow some latitude for those unexpected things that cannot be planned.

☑ Money

The funds necessary for a project will depend on the quality, quantity and available resources. Spend time mapping out the entire project and the possible related costs. Draft several financial models, which will take into consideration several scenarios. By analyzing the options, the final budget can sometimes be a hybrid of previous drafts.

CREATE A BUDGET

In this final step, all the activities that have been identified can now be assessed with a monetary value. Two approaches can be used to decide the financial course of the project.

One, the total dollar amount may be predetermined at the outset of the project. If this is the case, spend time tapping into your internal resources, which can provide money, equipment, supplies, etc., in order to offset some of the expenses.

Good networking will provide some value savings if done properly. Many times, people wanting to be a part of a project may not have a talent or the time to contribute, but are able to provide funds towards the project. In any case, utilize all avenues of assistance.

The second approach is the project "need" will dictate the final budget within reason or certain parameters. In other words-, "This is what we need. Let's develop a budget to meet that need." Although this approach may not be as constricting as the first approach, responsible stewardship is critical. Christians are still bound by sound stewardship principles that employ common sense and practicality.

PLANNING TOOLS

There are many different methods for displaying project plans. The key to the planning process is to convey to those involved where they fit in the project and how their roles affect the project.

The array of planning tools can run the gamut from a simple calendar to a very comprehensive PERT logic diagram. The important thing to remember is use whatever works best to communicate the goals, objectives, activities and the timing necessary to complete the project.

Tools of the Trade

Simple List of Needs – Simply list all the necessary things that will be needed to identify the activities of a project. A good brainstorming session will serve to disclose the activities, which can look like a simple shopping list.

The Gantt chart – The Gantt chart involves grouping tasks together within several categories. This is reflected by bar graphs to show relationships. The visual advantage to this method is that anyone can see beginning points, milestones or checkpoints, related activities, people responsible for events; and relationships among people and activities.

Gantt Chart					
Activity Description	Jan	Feb	Mar	Apr	May
Locate Site	███████████				
Secure Permits			██████		
Purchase Supplies				██████████	

Chronological Project List – Draft a list of events, showing the individuals responsible for each event and the dates to begin and complete them. The items are listed in order of completion. Simply crossing off each event when it is completed provides an excellent tracking method. One advantage to this tool is that everyone can see their responsibility and when their task or activity is complete. This speaks to the ownership principle mentioned previously.

The Storyboard – The Storyboard allows the participants to visualize the planning process. The participants brainstorm and write down all of the components, tasks and activities necessary for a project individually on a piece of paper. Next, place the pieces of paper or 3" x 5" cards on a wall or board. Then step back and look for common tasks and/or activities under

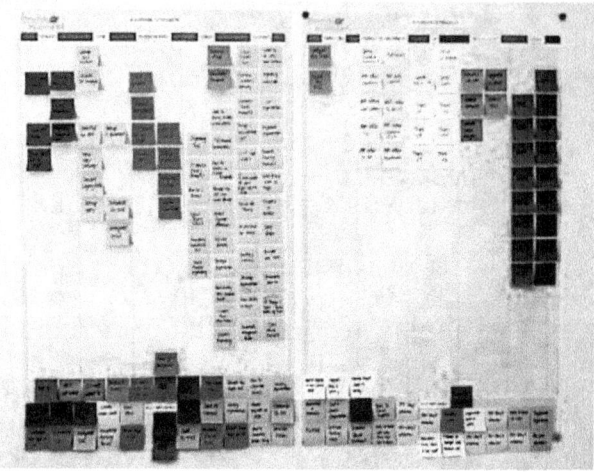

natural groupings or categories. Finally evaluate the entire process. Keep what makes sense and eliminate what doesn't fit.

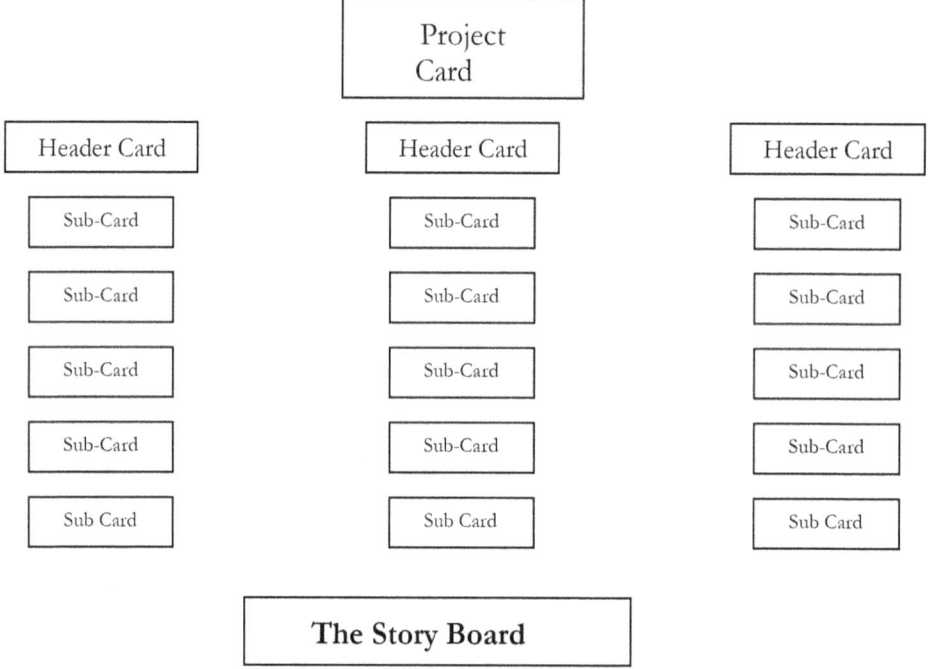

The Story Board

PERT logic diagram – This method ties one event to another. Each event relationally is tied to other events in time. Sequentially, any event to the left of another event must occur or be completed first before moving on to the next event. Moreover, logically, any event to the right happens after a particular event that preceded it. Drawing a line between the events that are related to each other show their relationships.

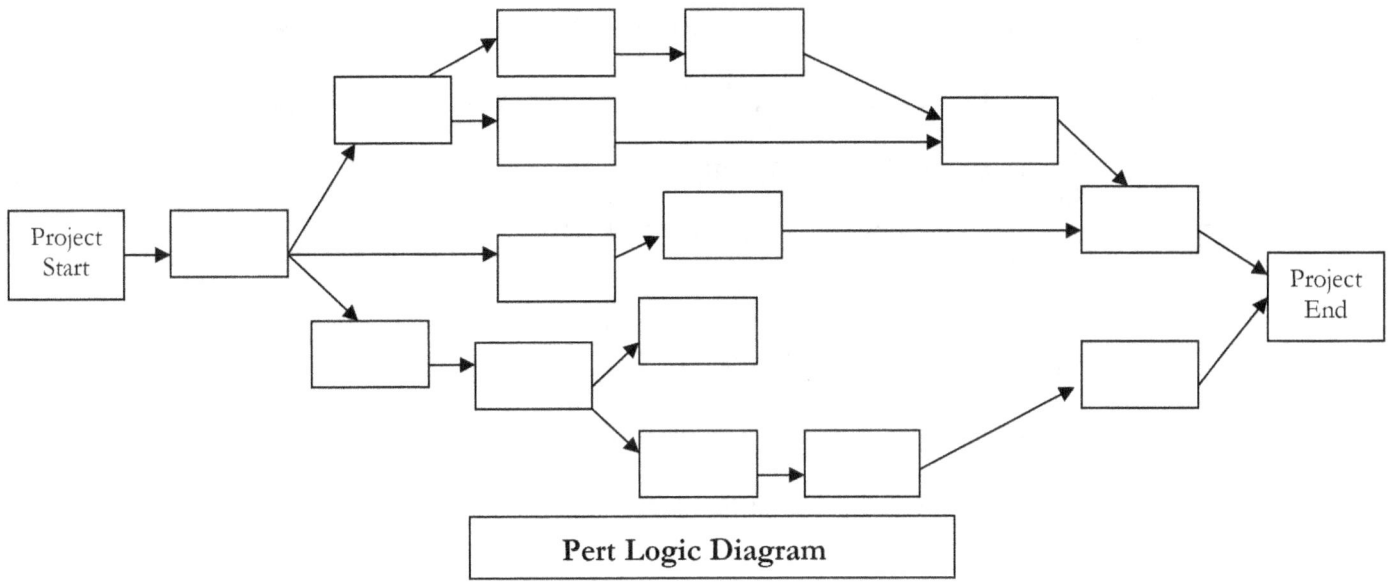

Pert Logic Diagram

SUMMARY

Planning is a key management role in any organization, whether a private business, a nonprofit organization, a corporate business or a government agency. Managers engage in different types of organizational planning to strategically steer their organizations towards profitable and successful futures.

The purpose of planning is to point the way from beginning to end. No plan will ever finish exactly as it was laid out initially. However, any plan should be viewed as a road map which will be periodically evaluated and adjusted as needed to reach the goal.

Ironically, many managers find the time to do a task or activity over again, but too often cannot find the time to plan right the first time! This is why it is vital to spend your time wisely. Efficient stewardship requires every manger to make the most of every resource and time sensitive activity.

Be mindful of the signs of poor planning, such as:

- Objectives and deadlines constantly not met

- Working feverishly in the eleventh hour to complete a task or project

- Vital resources such personnel, finances or facilities waiting to be used

- Doing the same task more than once.

Effective planning takes into consideration the following:

- Expect plans to change

- When you fail to plan, you plan to fail

- Whenever possible, have a contingency plan

Remember: Blessed are the flexible!

References:

1. Edward Dayton, Ted W. Engstrom, Strategy For Leadership, (Fleming H. Revell Co., 1979), page 77.

2. Myron Rush, *Management: A Biblical Approach*, (Wheaton, IL: Victor Books, 1985), pages 81-94.

PERSONAL APPLICAITON

1. Select a project and conduct a Storyboard exercise with you and others. Identify all the tasks and activities necessary to complete the project. Label them as either a "Heading" card to identify a major task or activity and or a "Sub-point" card for a supporting task or activity. Carefully distinguish between a major task (Heading card) and a supporting task (Sub-point).

2. Read Nehemiah, chapters 1 – 6. Answer the following questions:

   - What was the purpose of the project?

   - Why was it important?

   - Why was it a priority?

   - Was the purpose effectively communicated or did some not understand it?

   - How did Nehemiah manage adversity?

3. Conduct the Storyboard process to Nehemiah's project and create the "Topic", "Heading" and "Sub-"Sub-point" card to his project.

Organization

In the beginning God created the heavens and the earth. The earth was formless and void, and darkness was over the surface of the deep, and the Spirit of God was moving the surface of the waters. Genesis 1:1-2

God took what was confusion (formless) and organized matter into what we now know as our world. He was able to supernaturally bring order to something that had no order. Organizing atoms, neutrons, protons, electrons and the like, He created a vast array of complex forms of matter, including man.

Placing people and other resources into a structure to accomplish goals or objectives is one definition of "organization". You can just as easily define organization by what it is not:

- A rigid structure

- An unwanted system forced on unsuspecting people

- A restriction of freedom to get the job done

Organization is the complement to planning. The two functions go hand-in-hand. A similar analogy is that of knowledge and wisdom: "Knowledge comes by taking things apart, analysis. But wisdom comes by putting things together".[1] In retrospect, the

 following is true for planning and organization, the *Wisdom of* planning is being able to identify the purpose of a project or activity, and the *Knowledge* of organization is being able to pull together and sequence all the components to make the project or activity a reality.

When we speak of organization in the form of a noun, like a company, the following four concepts should be considered:

Process: An organization should be re-evaluated from time-to-time due to factors such as:

- Changing environment

- Organizational growth

- Turnover in personnel

People: Without people you have no organization. Don't get so wrapped up in organizational charts and job descriptions that you forget that you are working with real people. Be careful not overlook the human factor in organizing.

Structure: Like a skyscraper, which is under-girded by a frame of steel, so does an organizational structure serve to relate individuals to one another and provide the formal communicational lines necessary to any organization. Examples of structure are:

- organizational charts

- job descriptions

- company handbooks covering policies and procedures

Goals   The driving force in any organization should be to identify a vision and accomplish certain predetermined goals and objectives necessary in realizing the vision. To organize merely for the sake of organizing, without a clearly defined vision is meaningless.

WHY ORGANIZE?

If you do not organize, important things will be done ineffectively or not done at all. Such a problem occurred in the early church. In Acts 6:1-3, it is recorded that certain widows were overlooked in the daily serving of food. The problem was brought to the attention of the apostles. They, in turn, decided to assign certain qualified men to systematically handle the situation efficiently.

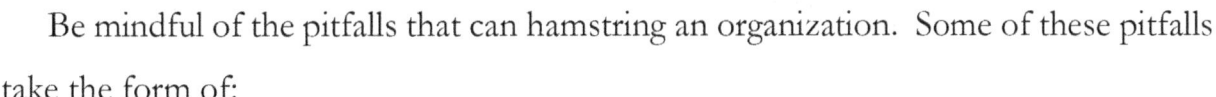

Be mindful of the pitfalls that can hamstring an organization. Some of these pitfalls take the form of:

- Too many meetings
- Too many or unnecessary approvals
- Indecision.

The "paralysis of analysis" as it's sometimes referred to, can hamper an organization and perpetuate frustration in everyone concerned. In any case, review procedures so that they make practical sense. Please note that often simplicity can be misconstrued as a lack of sophistication or maturity within an organization.

Remember, God honors organization, but it is important to realize that "organization" is merely a tool. Unless synchronicity is under pinned by God's Spirit, the organization will be ineffective at best. In Dr. Paulus Scharpff's book "History of Evangelism"[1], he states that John Wesley, Dwight L. Moody and John Mott, were outstanding examples of organization.

Below is an example of the nation of Israel's organization as they traveled in the wilderness. In order to move the Israelites, it was imperative that the leadership organize the people to minimize confusion. Note the presence of the Lord was at the center of His people.

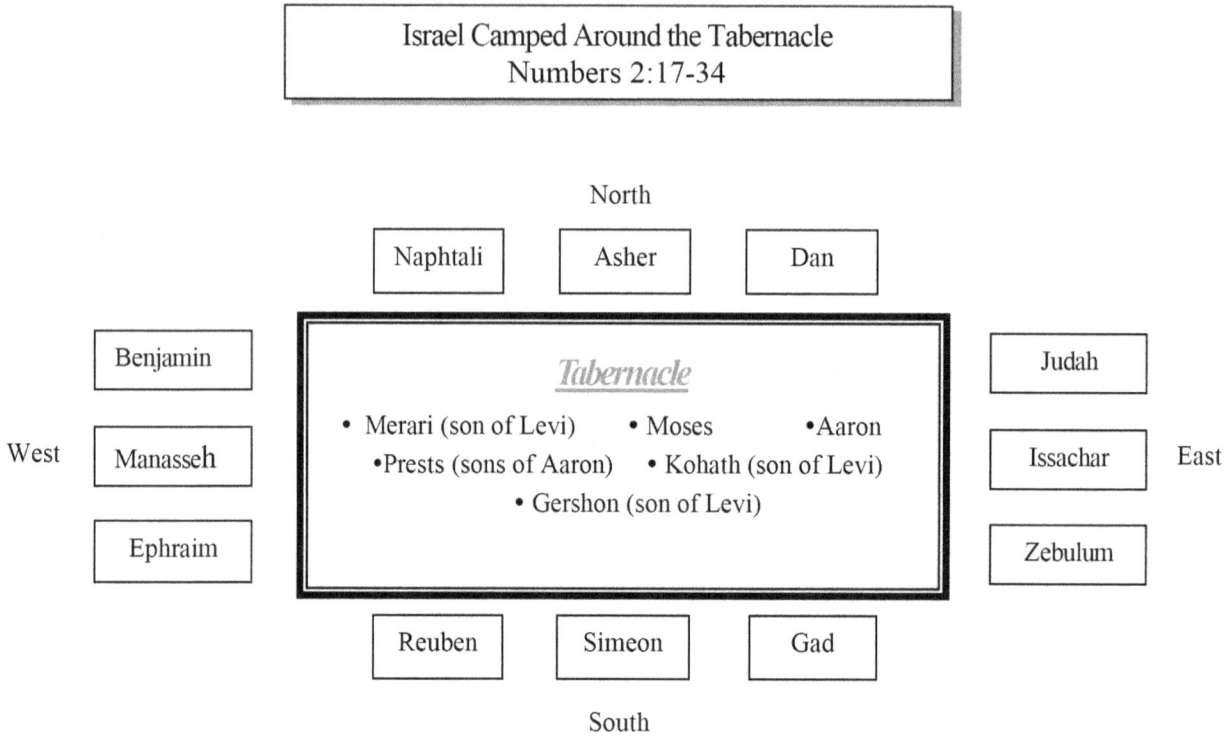

PRINCIPLES OF PROJECT ORGANIZATION

Use Strategy Before Structure – A common error is to begin to organize before you have determined what your goals and objectives are and how they relate to the plan.

Nehemiah exemplified this principle when he was given the vision to rebuild the Jerusalem wall.

> *". . . I did not tell anyone what my God was putting into my mind to do for Jerusalem . . . I went up at night . . . and inspected the wall . . . the wall of Jerusalem." Nehemiah 2:12, 15-17.*

Organize around natural groupings – In any planning, there tends to be "natural" clusters of activities and/or people that seem to go together. The activities that are the most similar and require the most intense and frequent interaction will need to be grouped together. Nehemiah employed this principle when he organized the people by family units in chapter three.

Be Specific – Assign definite assignments and responsibilities. Be deliberate in defining *who, what, where, why and when*, when tasking individuals. Nehemiah, in chapter three, defined job descriptions for his people and so did Moses in chapter three of the Book of Numbers, for the Levites.

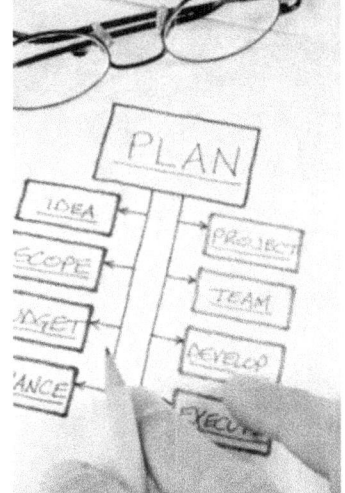

Without clear leadership and direction, confusion and frustration set in. Then as confusion and frustration begin to fester, apathy and dissension creeps in and ultimately torpedoes a project. After which, recovery is difficult and may deplete valuable resources.

Exercise Good Judgment in Selecting People for Leadership Roles

Prayerfully consider those who you will need to fulfill leadership roles to oversee key aspects of the project.

As you delegate responsibilities, look for individuals who are; trustworthy, proven, diligent and enthusiastic about the project. If these characteristics are not evident in an individual, then even the most skilled individual may lack buy-in and commitment. Subsequently, by making a simple statement like, "This is your goal.", you are essentially conveying to a person that he or she is responsible, and they can begin to know clearly where the parameters of the delegation lie.

ORGANIZATIONAL PRINCIPLES OF MANAGMENT

The four resources you organize within an organization are people, physical space, financial and information. As a manager you must organize your resources to achieve functional operating goals and objectives.

Henri Fayol (1841-1925) was a pioneer in administrative theory. He is known as the Pioneer of the Principles and Functions of Management. He also developed ten principles of organizational management[2]:

- Unity of command and direction

- Chain of command

- Span of management

- Division of labor

- Coordination

- Balanced responsibility and authority

- Delegation

- Flexibility

- Departmentalization

- Integration

For this module, we will cover only the following five these principles:

Unity of command and direction

Unity of command states that a subordinate should report only to one leader or manager. Unity of direction is when all activities are directed toward the same objective.

Unity of command minimizes confusion by avoiding overlapping leadership. Divided leadership can result in derailing someone's ability to prioritize responsibilities, activities and expectations.

Unity of command begins with the organization's mission. The mission will then drive all the activities throughout the entire strategic process. Moreover, as the strategic process develops, the organization begins to move towards achieving its vision.

Unity of Direction and Unity of Command Model

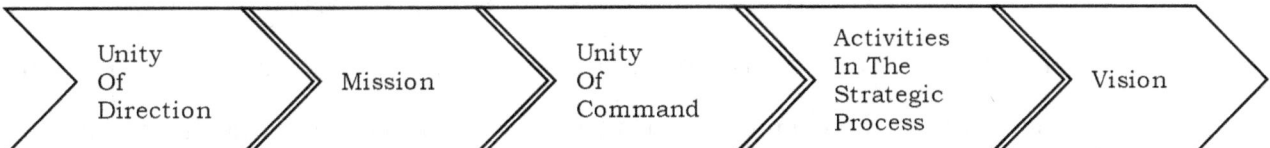

A working example of *Unity of Command* and *Unity of Direction* would be as follows:

An organization creates divisions with Managers to provide *Unity of Direction*. The division leaders then report to senior management. This now provides a *Unity of Command* for the divisions

Chain of Command

A straight line of authority from top to bottom best defines the *Chain of Command*. It defines who someone reports to and who reports to him or her. A well-known graphic visual illustrates the functionality of the *Chain of Command* is an organization chart. It contains vertical and horizontal levels which are based on authority and responsibilities.

The *Chain of Command* also serves as a formal communication tool. Associates within the organization generally handle affairs through chain of command. Actually, it is the preferred method within most organizations. However, sometimes it is necessary to work outside the chain of command; for example, when someone's leader or manager is unavailable or when dealing with ministries or departments outside of your own.

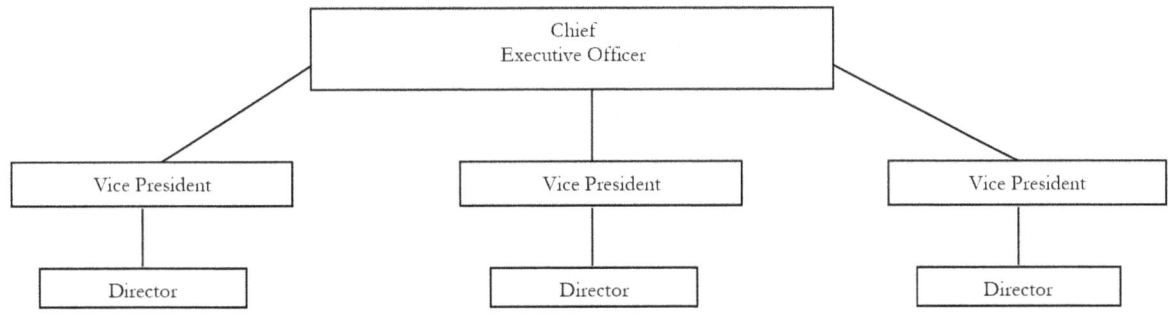

Span of Management

The *Span of Management* refers to the number of associates reporting to a manager or supervisor. The fewer direct reports the narrower the span becomes. Also, note that there is no "best" number of direct reports to oversee. Each reporting structure and Span of Management or Span of Control is unique.

Generally, lower-level managers will have a larger span of management than higher-level managers. A key for successful management is to limit the number to that which will be most effective and efficient. The proper span depends on the nature of work, management style, the abilities of the associates, personalities, goals, etc.

The positive factors of a wide span include delegation of authority, clear policies and positive behavior from associates who have more freedom. The positive factors of a narrower span include close supervision, control and fast communication.

Types of Organizational Levels:

A *flat organization*[3] is when only a few levels of management exist with wide spans of management control.

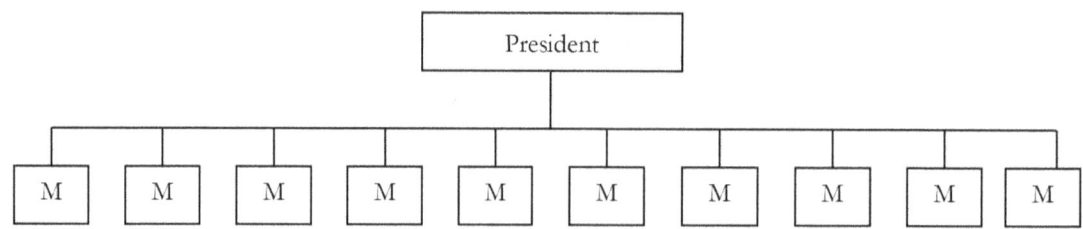

A *tall organization*[4] exists when there are several levels with narrow management control.

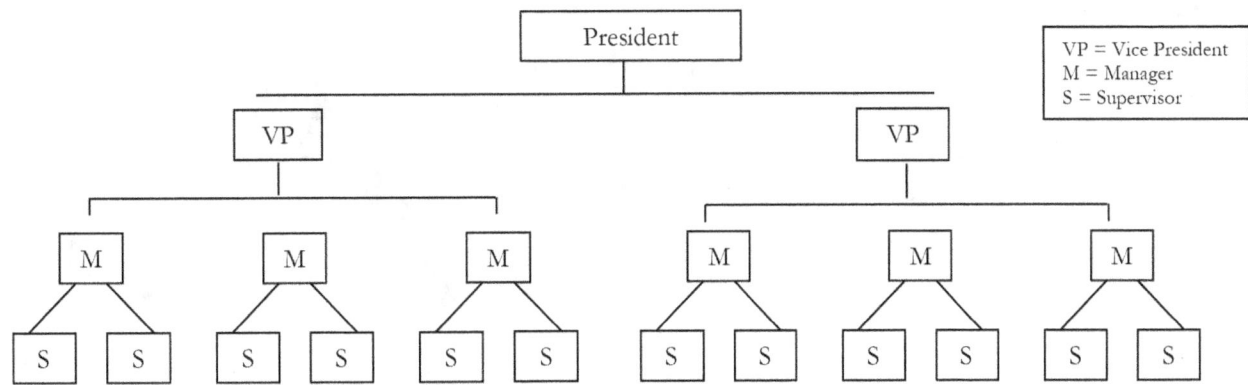

Coordination

Individuals, groups, or departments working together to accomplish the strategic and operational objectives of an organization is coordination in action. Coordination is the process of integrating organizational tasks and resources together to meet objectives. Conceptual skills are needed to aid an individual in succeeding to orchestrate all the resources available.

The tools needed to coordinate activities are unity of command and direction, chain of command, span of management, and balanced responsibility and authority. Listed below are other measures which can contribute to coordinating activities:

- Direct contact between people, groups and departments

- Liaisons within a group or department who coordinate information and activities for other groups or departments

- Committees made up of different group or department members who gather together to coordinate efforts.

Flexibility

There will always be exceptions to the rule; flexibility accommodates for such unpredictability. The tendency is to adhere to strict planning and organizing principles and ignore the needs of people or situations.

Flexibility helps to adjust and fulfill genuine unexpected needs when conventional practices say "no".

As good, as rules and regulations are, it is vital that exceptions to the rule be analyzed for what is practical. Otherwise, true needs that don't fit in a neat little box are overlooked or ignored.

HOW TO ORGANIZE

ORGANIZING HAS THREE COMPONENTS:

- Organizing from a plan
- Job descriptions
- Delegation

Organizing From A Plan

The following is a sequential list of steps in organizing the pertinent aspects of a project or creating an organizational structure:

A. List and prioritize activities that must be performed on a to-do-list, then;

- Assign each task a priority
- Identify natural groupings of activities that tend to naturally relate to one another
- Rank the order of performance

- Prioritize tasks, focus on accomplishing one task or a group of related tasks at a time

- Begin accomplishing each task by asking yourself three questions;

    1. *Do I need to be personally involved because of my unique knowledge and skills?* There are times when you are the only one that can do the task. But when practical, delegate the task to someone who is capable of completing the task.

    2. *Is the task within my major area of responsibility or will it affect the performance or finances of my group, ministry or department?* Many times, a simple yes or no will answer the question

    3. *Is a quick action needed?* Should you work on the activity right now or should you wait. The key is to start the task soon enough to meet the deadline.

B. Assign Priorities:

- After the three questions are answered,; a High, Medium or Low priority designation can be assigned, if delegation is necessary.

- *Delegate* – The task is delegated if the answer to question 1 is "no". At which point you must focus on selecting someone to complete the task.

    - *High* Priority - A high priority is assigned if you answer "yes" to all three questions.

    - *Medium* Priority - A medium priority is assigned if you answered "yes" to question 1, but "no" to questions 2 <u>or</u> 3.

    - *Low* Priority - A low priority is assigned if you answered "yes" to question 1, but "no" to questions 2 <u>and</u> 3.

C. Personnel

- List all available personnel

- Carefully slot people by their natural abilities and desires

- Allow for a little room to stretch the person in completing the task to aid in their growth

- Determine how much coaching the person will need. Set milestones for those who need more coaching than others

D. Develop an Organizational Chart

- Plot out the relationships of the people involved for clarity and accountability

- List three factors:

  - Name of the person

  - The line relationship to other people

  - The person assisting or supporting the person responsible

Job Descriptions

A typical "job descriptions" is a working document that describes the duties, responsibilities, level of accountability, working conditions, the physical demands and limitations which are essential for the position.

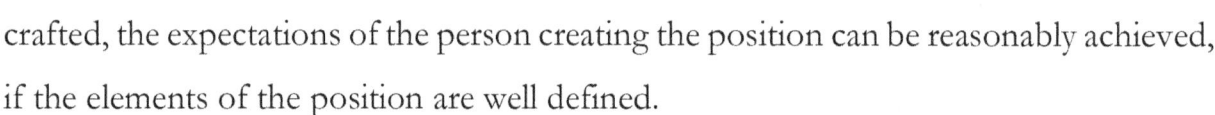

The job description is a tool for both the person assigning the task or position and the person who is expected to perform in a particular capacity. If the job description is carefully crafted, the expectations of the person creating the position can be reasonably achieved, if the elements of the position are well defined.

The following four questions should be answered in a job description:

1. What are the duties and responsibilities?
2. What authority does the position have?
3. To whom can the incumbent look for direction?
4. Who looks to the incumbent for direction?

The following are three terms that are significant to a job description:

1. Responsibility – the requirement of the position to perform assigned tasks, duties and obligations; and to meet expected performance results

2. Authority – the level at which the position has the right to make decisions

3. Accountability – the position's obligation to carry out assigned responsibilities and to be accountable for decisions made

Listed below are some guidelines for writing a job description:

- State the title of the job

- Determine the overall purpose of the job. The purpose should be stated in brief summary

- State the scope of the job. The scope refers to the functional boundaries of the job

- List the specific responsibilities of the job and all that it encompasses

- List the working relationships. Show the following:

  This position reports to: _____

  Reporting directly to the position: _____

  The position works closely with: _____

Delegation

Delegation is defined as the practice of assigning responsibility and authority in order to accomplish a task(s) or objective(s). It means giving another person or persons a certain degree of discretion that's not inherent in their role--the right to make decisions that are officially tied to your role and for which you are ultimately responsible.

As an example of delegation, some secular organizations, as a part of their "employee empowerment programs," delegate quite a bit of decision-making authority to their employees in order to promote employee spontaneity for the sake of customer service, quality or innovation.

"Delegation" will be covered in more detail in the "Delegation" module. Areas such as benefits and obstacles of delegation will be discussed.

SUMMARY

Organization is a complement to planning. The two functions work in tandem in coordinating the initial efforts of any project. Setting an order or a sequence of events provides the map of the logical steps in arriving at a goal. By not taking the time to organize, important things will be done ineffectively or not all.

There are four basic areas, which are organized within a project; people, tangible resources, money and information. Avoid the common error of beginning to organize before you determine what your goals and objectives are, and how they relate to the plan. Specifically, identify the purpose before setting out on the rest of the process.

Planning must be placed more in the hands of those responsible for executing the plan, rather than in the hands of designers.[5] If this is not possible, then the function of organization must be placed in the hands of synthesizers. In other words, people who can bring harmony and order in orchestrating each aspect of a project.

In I Corinthians, Paul provides for us an illustration of the perils of "dis-organization" in the church.

> *What is {the outcome} then, brethren? When you assemble, each one has a psalm, has a teaching, has a revelation, has a tongue, and has an interpretation. Let all things be done for edification. If anyone speaks in a tongue, {it should be} by two or at the most three, and {each} in turn, and let one interpret; but if there is no interpreter, let him keep silent in the church; and let him speak to himself and to God. And let two or three prophets speak, and let the others pass judgment. But if a revelation is made to another who is seated, let the first keep silent. For you can all prophesy one by one, so that all may learn and all may be exhorted; and the spirits of prophets are subject to prophets; for God is not {a God} of confusion but of peace, as in all the churches of the saints.*
> *1 Corinthians 14:26-33 (NAS)*

References:

1. John Morrison, The Role of Religion in Education, as cited in Baude's Handbook of Stories for Toastmasters and Speakers (1975), 194.

2. Paulus Scharpff, History of Evangelism; Three Hundred Years of Evangelism in Germany, Great Britain, and the United States, Helga Bender Henry, tr. – Grand Rapids: Eerdmans, 1966.

3. Robert N. Lussier, Management: Concepts, Applications and Skill Development, (Cincinnati, OH; South-Western College Publishing, 1997), page 20,77.

4. Ibid, page 210.

5. Ibid, page 210.

6. Ted W. Engstrom, Your Gift of Administration, (Nashville, TN; Thomas Nelson, Inc., 1983), page 103.

7. Op. cit., Management: Concepts, Applications and Skill Development, page 228.

PERSONAL APPLICATON

1. Create an organizational chart. You may design a chart from any organization in which you are personally involved with, such as your; church, place of employment, club, etc..

2. Assume the role of a ministry leader who is in charge of planning and implementing a community evangelistic outreach. Use the task matrix[5] below to develop all of the tasks and activities necessary to complete the project. List them sequentially and prioritize them. The first task has been prioritized as an example. Use a separate sheet of paper if you need additional lines.

Assigning A Priority	Task Qualifying Questions				Priority
D – Delegate priority = (N) No to question 1 H – High priority = (YYY) Yes to all three questions M – Medium priority = (YNY or YYN) Yes to questions 1 and 2 or 3 L – Low priority = (YNN) Yes to question 1 and No to questions 2 and 3 **Task**	1. Do I Need to be involved?	2. Am I personally responsible for this task or effect the over project?	3. Does this task need to be turned around quickly?	Deadline date	
Set up chairs for Easter Sunrise service (example event)	N	Y	Y	3/23	H

Delegation

Now after this the Lord appointed seventy others, and sent them in pairs ahead of Him to every city and place where He himself was going to come. Luke 10:1

When our Lord commissioned the seventy disciples to go out, He was not delegating His authority as a personal convenience. He purposely selected these men as an opportunity to develop them and advance the gospel through them. His delegation was no small act. In verse nineteen of the same chapter written above, Luke discloses that He delegated authority to tread on serpents, scorpions and over all the power of the enemy. Not only were they empowered with responsibility but authority. The key in this aspect of delegation is matching the right person to the right job.

After prioritizing tasks within a project, the ability to assess what you must do and what others can do, can be a challenge for someone who struggles with control. Following the prioritizing of tasks, ask yourself some basic questions regarding your level of involvement in the activities of the project:

- Do I need to get personally involved, because of my unique skills or experience; yes or no? This critical question may challenge your comfort zone.

- Is this task within my major realm of responsibility, yes or no? This question asks, "Does this task have a direct or significant impact on the project's budget or outcome?" If the answer is yes, then you must consider one of two options. One, oversee the activity to completion yourself. Or two, appoint someone who is trustworthy and able to complete it under your specific direction.

- When is the deadline? Is a quick action necessary; yes or no? A decision should be based on whether the task or a project step needs to start now; or can it wait? The key is to start the task with ample time to avoid missing a deadline.

BENEFITS AND OBSTACLES OF DELEGATION

Several *benefits* point to the efficiency of delegation:

! DELEGATE !

- More time can be directed on higher priority tasks[1]
- Spreading responsibilities increases the potential of successfully accomplishing tasks and increases productivity[2]
- It serves as a great tool to train people for future responsibilities and increase confidence[3]
- It provides an avenue for reducing a manager's stress and burden[4]

Some *obstacles* which will prevent a manager from utilizing the delegation process include:

- Refusing to release control because they are accustomed to doing things themselves[5]
- Fearing that people will fail to complete the task assigned[6]
- Fearing that someone will perform better then themselves
- Convinced that they can perform the tasks more efficiently than others[7]
- Lacking the knowledge of "what" to delegate or "how" to delegate

3-PRONGED DELEGATION

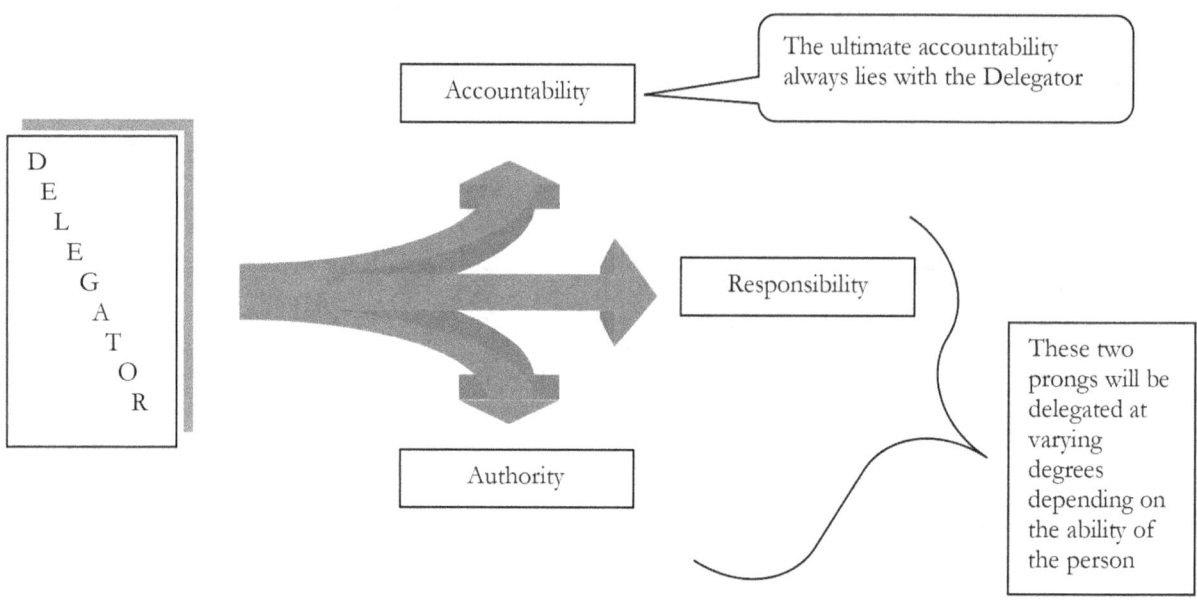

DELEGATION GUIDELINES

Two key decisions must be made

What to delegate?

Whom to delegate to?

What to delegate?

One method that will aid you in assessing priorities is a "to-do" list. List all the tasks involved in a project. Write them down in no particular order. Mentally walk through everything that needs to happen to successfully accomplish a task or tasks necessary to meet an objective or deadline.

Spend some time considering what you personally <u>do not</u> have to get involved with to complete the task or project. Analyze where your unique talents or skills can be best utilized in the bigger picture of a project. **Learn to let go!**

For example, here are some areas that can be delegated-[8]

- *Routine tasks:* Tasks such as ordering, checking schedules, phone calls, etc.

- *Paperwork:* Delegate memo writing, communication pieces, reports, etc.

- *Tasks that can develop others:* Give others an opportunity to learn and grow

    - Prepare them for larger responsibilities in areas such as:

        - Solving problems: Teach others to solve their own problems. Encourage them to utilize critical thinking, with your coaching as support.

        - Technical problems: Assign more qualified people to support those who are less qualified to answer and resolve problems.

What not to delegate?

Keep those activities that require your particular talents and unique skills.

Here are some areas that <u>should not</u> be delegated-[9]

- Personnel tasks such as counseling, appraisals, conflict resolutions, disciplining, disciplinary actions, etc.

- Confidential matters

- Crisis – most often, there is no time to delegate

- Activities delegated to you personally by someone else.

Whom To Delegate To?

Know, within reason, the ability of the person being delegated the task. Consider the person's talents, ability, strengths, sort-comings, and commitment. Ask yourself the question, "Can this person get the job done by the deadline?"

Two very important points to practice once the decision is made to delegate to someone:

1. Meet with the person selected for the task or project

   This is the time you take to explain all the aspects of the task or project such as instructions, requirements, and special factors associated with the task or project. Also, this is where you cover such things as:

   - When the assignment begins

   - All instructions for completing the project

   - How much authority is being delegated in order to make decisions

   - What resources are available to aid the person (people, supplies, equipment, etc.).

   - Discuss any special considerations of the task or project

   - Who the delegated person goes to for assistance and accountability

   - The purpose of the project and its importance

   - Most importantly, clearly disclose your expectations for completing the task(s) or project

2. Follow up with the person on the progress:

   - Misunderstood instructions early in the process lay the foundation for costly mistakes, in both time and resources. The assumption is that everything was communicated successfully cannot be totally relied upon

- Take an active role in establishing milestones to monitor progress to ensure the task or project is on target.

The lower the capability of the person, the more important it is to follow up. Develop a feedback system that will satisfy your comfort level and not undermine the person's confidence.

Set objectives so that the level of responsibility, authority and accountability is clearly understood. Be specific as to the expectations during the task, the deadline and what the successful results should be.

This is Delegation!

This is NOT Delegation!

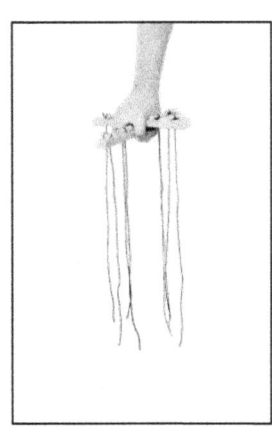

BIBLICAL CASE STUDY

It came about the next day that Moses sat to judge the people, and the people stood about Moses from the morning until the evening.

Now when Moses' father-in-law saw all that he was doing for the people, he said, "What is this thing that you are doing for the people? Why do you alone sit as judge and all the people stand about you from morning until evening?"

Moses said to his father-in-law, "Because the people come to me to inquire of God. When they have a dispute, it comes to me, and I judge between a man and his neighbor and make known the statues of God and His laws.

Moses' father-in-law said to him, "The thing that you are doing is not good". You will surely wear out both yourself and these people who are with you, for the task is too heavy for you; you cannot do it alone.

Now listen to me: I shall give you counsel, and God be with you, You be the people's representative before God, and you bring the disputes to God, then teach them the statues and the laws, and make known to them the way in which they are to walk and the work they are to do.

Furthermore, you shall select out of all the people able men who fear God, men of truth, those who hate dishonest gain; and you shall place these over them as leaders of thousands, of hundreds, of fifties and tens.

"Let them judge the people at all times; and let it be that every major dispute they will bring to you, but every minor dispute they themselves will judge. So it will be easier for you, and they will bear the burden with you."

"If you do this thing and God so commands you, then you will be able to endure, and all these people also will go their place in peace."

So Moses listened to his father-in-law and did all that he had said. Moses chose able men out of all Israel and made them heads over the people, leaders of thousands, of hundreds, of fifties and of tens. They judged the people at all times; the difficult dispute they would bring Moses, but every minor dispute they themselves would judge. Exodus 18:13-26 (NAS)

Moses recognized the value of wise counsel. He realized that it was not only jeopardizing his own well-being, but also risking the possibility of frustrating the people. By distributing the load among qualified men, he demonstrated trust in their judgment and bolstered their confidence.

Some control-oriented managers will point out that Moses had capable people in which to delegate, thereby using an excuse not to delegate themselves. As a result, they keep the work to themselves. However, upon closer inspection, the only recent job on the résumé of the men Moses selected was brick making. The key criteria in selecting these men were honesty and trust. With these attributes as a foundation, Moses was willing to take a risk by developing them and sharing his leadership.

Depth and Breadth of a Leader's Ability

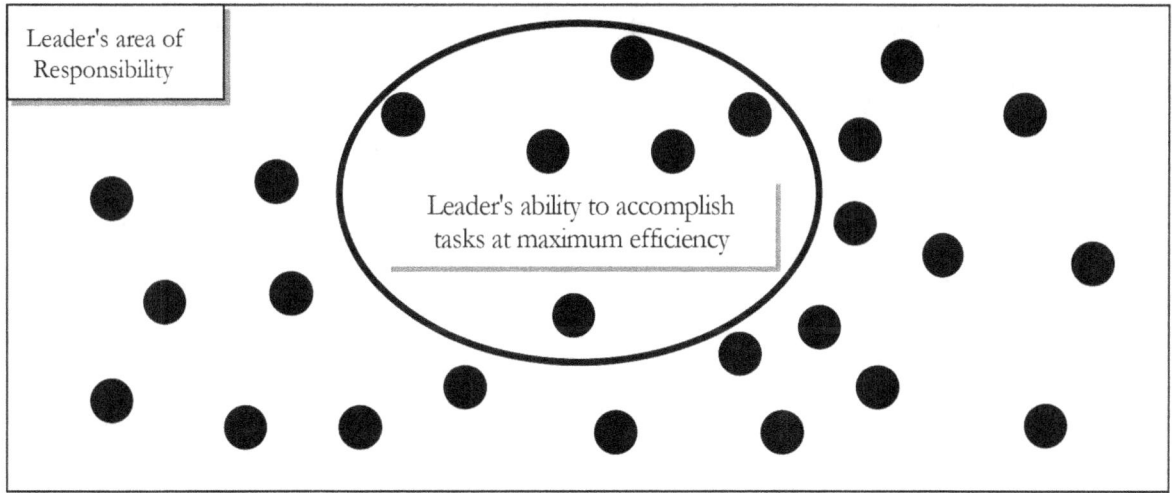

Leader's area of Responsibility

Leader's ability to accomplish tasks at maximum efficiency

DELGATION BARRIERS [11]

1. ***"The task or project will not be done the way I would do it"***

   The fear or uncertainty that someone else will not do it your way speaks volumes about your need to control everything. Yes, there is a risk that the person or persons may not accomplish a task or activity as you would. However, if you, the one delegating, match the right people to the task, then more than likely the outcome may be better

2. ***"My subordinates lack the training to perform the task adequately"***

   In making this statement, the leader overlooks his or her own failure in developing people. Delegation is the most effective and least expensive way to train people.

3. ***"I really like to do it all, therefore there is no reason to delegate"***

   Leaders tend to gravitate to the familiar, especially when they are new to managing people and projects. Leaders must strive to separate themselves to allow others to grow.

All three of the barriers listed above contain one common element, "I". The inability to see beyond oneself will always be a hindrance. It is so easy to go to the familiar and take matters into your own hands. One re-occurring reason is that leaders who wrestle with delegation may feel they are losing control. This concern can be overcome by setting well thought out parameters and expectations that identify the boundary lines.

The inability to "let go" does not have to be a chronic or incurable condition. However, if you find yourself with not enough time to finish everything, experiencing extraordinary mental and physical fatigue, spending more time in an operational role rather than a strategic role, these may signs of obsessive behavior.

From time-to-time stop and evaluate your current role and workload. Review your calendar and current project list and ask yourself some deliberate and thought-provoking questions, such as:

- Is there a balance between my free time and my committed time?

- What are the tasks or activities that only "I" can really do?

- What tasks or activities can I truly delegate to someone with some coaching, a little coaching or no coaching?

- Are there tasks or activities that can be collapsed into other tasks or activities?

HOW TO OVERCOME THE BARRIERS TO DELEGATION

Many managers' attitudes and beliefs interfere with their use of effective delegation. Check the statements below against reality.

"Delegation is abdication." Proper delegation isn't anything like abdication, it's actually hard work. Of course, dumping tasks on your subordinates without a systematic approach to fostering their success and **skill development** is abdication. However, there are many legitimate business reasons to delegate.

"Delegating would mean giving up power and control." Not when done properly. Effective delegation involves retaining control over the work output. Only decisions about processes can be totally turned over to subordinates. Furthermore, by you delegating, managers leverage their subordinates' efforts to become more productive and influential themselves. In addition,

delegating frees up time that can use to pursue innovative projects. If you can't think of several innovative projects that you could pursue with some free time, then a lack of creativity is your problem, not delegating.

"Delegating makes me nonessential." Do you fear that your subordinates are "gaining on you"? Do you think the best way to deal with that fear is to hold them back? If so, see a therapist, because that's a recipe for failure due to paranoia. Your subordinates and your ministry or organization appreciate a manager who can develop and empower subordinates. Again, delegating frees up time that you can use to pursue innovative projects that make you valuable to your organization.

"Delegating is not worth the time. I can do the job myself faster and better." That's shortsighted. If you don't delegate tasks because you want to save time in the short run, there is a likelihood that, in the future, when you are overloaded with work, you may not have fellow ministry workers or staff that's prepared to help you.

"I can't count on my fellow ministry workers or staff to handle this." If you're not giving them the chance, how would you know? If you delegate incrementally and continually, your fellow ministry workers or staff will acquire the necessary capabilities. Let them learn from their mistakes like you did when you first learned how to perform the task. If your subordinates are not

encouraged to continually learn new skills and information, you need to counsel them. And, if they are motivated to learn, coach them.

SUMMARY

King David in Psalm 8:3-9 (NASB), gives us an example of God's attitude towards delegation:

"When I consider Your heavens, the works of Your fingers,

The moon and the stars, which You have ordained;

What is man that You take thought of him,

And the son of man that You care for him?

Yet You have made him a little lower than God,

And You crown him with glory and majesty!

You make him to rule over the works of your hands;

You have put all things under his feet,

All sheep and oxen,

And also the beasts of the field,

The birds of the heavens and the fish of the sea,

Whatever passes through the paths of the seas.

O Lord, Our Lord, How majestic is Your name in all the earth!"

God entrusted His creation to the dominion of man. And although man forfeited this privilege when he sinned in the garden, today we continue to have a limited responsibility of that delegated task.

If we say we strive to emulate our Lord in all things, then some thought has to be given to how we should include others whenever possible. Our Lord could have easily put us in a very structured environment so that He could control everything. Certainly it isn't impossible for Him to be everywhere at all times. But, it is for us! We need to look for opportunities to share God's calling for us with others. As a result, this may reveal opportunities for them to explore and develop their calling in His service.

"Goal setting utilizes the concept of delegation and mutual agreement on what has been delegated".[11]   By communicating to the person you are delegating the intended goal or task, you are conferring responsibility and ownership.   And, as reinforcement, clearly disclose the parameters to ensure a successful outcome.   This by no means implies a guarantee in successfully completing a task or project. However, it will develop an environment of cooperation, trust and ownership.   These are elements which cannot be nurtured in an autocratic ministry.

The bottom line is that strategic delegation takes time, and for many of us, it requires overcoming our personal barriers to delegating.   However, it is well worth the effort.   By delegating effectively, you get your fellow ministry workers or staff engaged in important and challenging work, you allow them to develop their skills and prepare for the next level of responsibility, and clear your schedule so that you can work on innovative projects.

References:

1.   "Delegation: It's Often a Problem for Agency Owners", Agency Sales Magazine, May 1995, Vol. 25, Iss. 5, pp.35-38

2.   Ted Pollock, "Secrets of Successful Delegation", Production, December 1994, Vol. 106, Iss. 12, pp. 10-12

3.   Jack Ninemeier, "10 Tips for Delegating Task", Hotels, June 1995, Vol. 29, Iss. 6, pp. 20-21

4.   Op cit, Jack Ninemeir

5.   Ibid, "Delegation: It's Often A Problem For Agency Owners", Agency Sales Magazine

6.   Ibid, Ted Pollock, "Secrets of Successful Delegation"

7.   Rebecca Morgan, "Guidelines For Delegating Effectively", Supervision, April 1995, Vol. 56, Iss. 4, pp. 20-22

8.   Robert N. Lussier, Management: concepts, applications and skill development, (Cincinnati, OH; South-Western College Publishing, 1997), page 230

9.   Op cit

10. Myron Rush, Management: A Biblical Approach, 1983, SP Publications, Victor Books, Wheaton IL, page 138

11. Ibid, page 148

12. Edward R. Dayton and Ted W. Engstrom, Strategy For Leadership, 1979, Fleming A. Revell

    Company, page 67

PERSONAL APPLICATION

1. Review the illustration regarding the "Depth and breath of a leader's ability" and identify activities that are inside and outside <u>your</u> scope as they apply to your job or current ministry.

2. List these activities and track them for two weeks. Look for changes, patterns, or trends that may help you to identify activities which you can possibly delegate.

3. Next, review the delegation guidelines and begin identifying a person or persons that you can pass some of these responsibilities to.

4. Make sure that the parameters are clearly defined, and responsibilities are fully understood.

5. Create a log of the progress of each delegated task or activity.

6. Re-evaluate and then correct as needed.

Communication

And when I came to you, brethren, I did not come with superiority of speech or of wisdom, proclaiming to you the testimony of God. I Corinthians 2:1

Paul, in the passage above clearly understood one the the basic principles of communication- keep it simple. Yes, there are times when our audience is sophisticated enough to understand "lofty" words and conepts. However, we must ask ourselves, "are we communicating in this manner to impress or is it entirely appropriate for this particular audience?" This is especially true when communicating the gospel.

The vocabulary we use is not the only thing to take into consideration as we interact with others. An effective communicator will attempt to understand such things as culture, unique sensitivities, current events, history, social issues and so on, before addressing an audience. Taking the extra steps to know your audience increases your chances of successfully commuicating your message.

The process we go through to convey ideas or understanding from one person or group to another [1] is one definition of communication. The key in this definition is "understanding". Hence, when someone complains about poor communication or lack of it, it may be due to a deficiency in *understanding*.

In Matthew, chapter thirteen, Jesus communicates a variety of topics in the form of parables. However, he doesn't take it for granted that His message is being understood, he actually asks for feedback by saying . . .

"Have you understood all these things? And, they said to Him, "Yes".
Matthew 13:51 (NASB)

Our Lord was aware of the importance of reaching His audience. If His message was not being understood, no matter how well He preached or how long, He would not have been communicating effectively if they had not understand His message.

This is still true today in ministry. Imagine a pastor delivering his sermons week-after-week thinking his congregation is grasping the essentials of his message only to find out that most everyone is lost because he spoke over their heads. Although the illustration may be a bit overstated, the point is that there is a heavy burden on the transmitter of the message, which requires soliciting feedback from the receiver in order to ensure a successful transmission of what is being communicated.

Picture a young child (transmitter) in the yard tossing a ball at a "pitch back" apparatus. The ball flies through the air, hits the mesh screened apparatus (receiver), and bounces back with the same force.

The illustration above and to the right is the complete cycle of successful communication. The message is sent out by the transmitter (encode), the receiver captures (decode) the message, interprets the message and provides "feedback" to the transmitter. Thus, completing the cycle and assuring the message is understood.

Effective Communication Cycle

Message
Encode
Send
Decode
Interpret
Feedback

Below is a technical illustration of communication [2]

The Roles and Responsibilities of Communication

Transmitters	Receivers
• Initiates the communication • Considers the Receiver and their processing needs • Organizes the information for the Receiver to understand • Selects the communication tool, i.e., face-to-face, mail, telephone, etc. • Provides feedback options if necessary • Responsible for the communication successfully being understood	• Decodes the communication by translating into meaningful content and understanding • After translating the communication, the Receiver evaluates it for effectiveness • Evaluates whether feedback is necessary or not • Selects the communication tool, i.e., face-to-face, mail, phone, etc., if feedback required

SIX STEPS IN THE COMMUNICATION PROCESS

The preceding graphic illustration can be summarized into six steps. The first three steps are for the person transmitting the communication and the last three steps are for the person receiving the communication. [2]

Transmitter:

1. Develop a clear concept of the idea or feeling to be communicated

2. Choose the right words and actions to communicate the right idea and/or feeling

3. Become aware of the surrounding communication barriers and work at minimizing them

Receiver:

1. Absorb the transmitted information by listening to the words and observing the actions

2. Translate the words into actions

3. Develop correct ideas and/or feelings

THE SIGNIFICANCE OF EFFECTIVE COMMUNICAITON

Genesis 11:1-9 gives an example of how communication played an integral part in accomplishing a goal. Although the hearts of the people were not inline with God's heart, it took the Lord's intervention to stop the building.

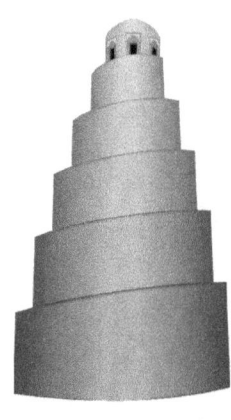

Verse 1 illustrates an important ingredient that is needed in successful communication: "Now the whole earth used the same language and the same words." Everyone was on the same page with one language, same dictionary, etc. However, today even though we may speak the same language, the words we use may mean something different when we express ourselves. For example, does the word "bad" mean something less than good or does it mean something really cool or great!

In Genesis 11:6, the Lord confirms that because of their common language, the people were united in completing a common goal. In seeing their united efforts succeeding, it motivated them even more to further push for a successful completion. This emphasizes the point that good communication can stimulate a person or group to be creative, innovative, and determined.

The Lord acknowledged the effectiveness of their plans by short-circuiting their most important tool- communication.

"Come, let Us go down and there confuse their language, that they may not understand one another's speech." Genesis 11:7

In order to destroy their productivity, the Lord had to strike at the heart of the project. As a result, by confusing their language, the people were scattered throughout the world, and the project was abandoned.

The significance of this scripture as it relates to communication is the critical role it plays in getting things done. The clear flow of ideas, innovations, articulation of strategies and goals, motivation all depend on effective communication, which can be encoded and decoded into a meaningful message. Otherwise, confusion, frustration, apathy, and discouragement derail even the best of intentions.

METHODS OF COMMUNICATION

Oral	Nonverbal	Written
Face-to-face	Setting	Memos
Meetings	Body language	Letters
Presentations	Pictures	Reports
Telephone		Newsletters
Voicemail		E-mail

KNOW THE COMMUNICATIONS BARRIERS

- Tuning people out and only hearing what we want to hear

- Allowing personal emotions to distort the message

- A lack of trust in the other person's motives

- Noise or other distractions

- Differing value systems and perceptions

- Unwillingness to receive information that conflicts with predetermined convictions or viewpoints

- Words that have several different meanings

- People's actions not corresponding to what is being said

KEYS TO MINIMIZING BARRIERS

It is unrealistic to believe that all communication will be 100% successful in transmission or reception. However, by recognizing the obstacles and practicing some simple techniques listed below, anyone can increase their success rate substantially.

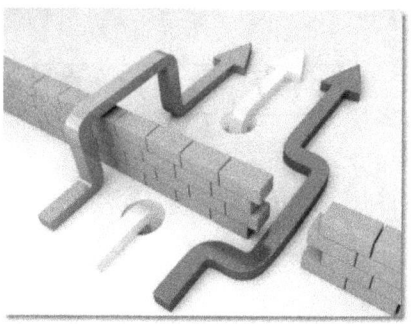

- Whenever possible, use face-to-face communication

- Use direct simple words (don't try to impress people with your vocabulary)

- Solicit feedback from the listener

- Give full attention to the speaker

- Never interrupt the speaker (who is not ready to listen to you until they have said what they are thinking or feeling). Encourage freedom of expression (agree to disagree, be willing to be open to the other person's ideas or feelings)

VALUE OF LISTENING

In a management study conducted by Management Training Systems, it was revealed that poor listening was the cause for most misunderstanding. According to Myron Rush[3], the president of Management Training Systems, in Colorado

Springs, Colorado, 45% of our waking day is spent listening. In addition, unless people have specific training, the efficiency of this listening skill is only 25%.

The difficulty lies in the fact that the average person can listen at a rate of 400 to 600 words per minute. In contrast, most people can only speak 200 to 300 words per minute. Consequently, our minds tend to look for something else to occupy our time while we are listening. This results in inattentive listening and missing essential data or feelings that are being conveyed.

With a little work and effort, anyone can improve their listening skills. The following principles provide valuable direction for improving the lines of communication with a moderate amount of effort.[4]

- Do not be afraid to ask questions for clarification. This is a common mistake because listeners are embarrassed. It is always better to ask early in the conversation rather than later.

- Do not start to develop a response, until the speaker is finished – You lose concentration while the speaker is talking, and a misunderstanding begins to formulate.

- Avoid preconceived impressions or attitudes about the speaker's subject matter – False or misguided assumptions are difficult to correct after the facts are presented. Moreover, it may result in only hearing what we want to hear

- .Avoid interrupting the speaker – There is a time to speak and a time to be silent, Solomon tells us in Ecclesiastes 3:7. Learn to be patient and "hear" what is actually being said. You will have plenty of time to evaluate the information before conclusively forming an opinion.

- Listen to the ideas and feelings behind the words – some studies show that only about 7% of a message is communicated in spoken words. The other 93% is communicated by tone of voice or some other non-verbal action or expression.

CHRISTIAN PRINCIPLES OF COMMUNICATION

In today's world, information and communication is constantly changing our environment. More and more we see that public communication tends to create dividing lines. We see an ever-increasing division between the "Have's and Have-not's", the oppressed and the free and distorted information which furthers the cause of many self-serving people and organizations. We especially see this subversive agenda in the media which manipulates information for the sake of sensationalism, hidden agendas, increasing market share and the bottom line.

However, communication continues to be a vital component in God's plan for His people. Communication provides us insight into the nature of God through His Word. The mere fact that we have a holy and anointed revelation of God through the scriptures implies God's desire to communicate with us.

Through communication we benefit from our interaction with other people, communities, and social orders of diverse cultures and lifestyles. Communication allows us to bridge the gap of ignorance due to the lack of understanding each other. As we continue to explore our world, it is imperative that we continue to develop and enhance how we communicate if we are to win people to Christ.

What sets "Christian" and secular communication principles apart is the eternal perspective. The basis of "Christian" communication principles is the "Good News for the Kingdom". These principles promote a common methodology and expression of how to effectively send and receive the transforming power of God and His nature.

Communication from a "Christian" Perspective

Jesus announced the coming of God's Kingdom and commissioned us to proclaim the "Good News" to all people until the end of time. Hearing the "Good News", living by it and witnessing to it, is the basic calling of all Christians. To enable us to carry out this task, we have been promised the power of the Holy Spirit. It is this Spirit that can change the "Babel" of confusion into the "Pentecost" of genuine understanding. But the Spirit 'blows where it pleases' (John 2:8), and no one, neither church nor religious group, can claim to control it.

The "Good News" addresses itself to the whole person and to all people. We pray for the coming of the Kingdom as well as for our daily food, for God's reign is in the world-to-come and the here-and-now. For Christian communicators, the material and the spiritual are part of each other. Christ's own communication was an act of self-giving. "He emptied himself, taking the form of a servant". (Phil 2:7). He ministered to all, but took up the cause of the materially poor, the mentally ill, and the outcasts of society, the powerless and oppressed. In the same way, Christian communication should be an act of love which liberates all who take part in it.

The Gospel, being the "Good News" for the poor, needs to be constantly reinterpreted from the perspectives of the poor and oppressed. This challenges church hierarchies to disassociate themselves from the power structures which keep the poor in a position of subservience. In this sense, the "Good News" for the poor embodies genuine reconciliation by means of which the dignity of all people can be reaffirmed.

By accepting Christ's sovereignty, the Christian communicator proclaims God's Kingdom rather than our divided churches. The churches do not exist for their own sakes, but for the sake of the Kingdom. For this reason, the Christian communicator gives preference to evangelical communication so that Christians of different denominations can speak with one voice, thus bearing witness to the one body of Christ.

Christian communicators, as witnesses to the Kingdom, should awaken and reflect the corporate witness of the church. The lives of Christians, as well as the work of communicators, need to be set free from the individualism which characterizes some cultures and traditions. We need to rediscover the early Christian community's understanding of witnessing and communicating the gospel.

The church as a community of believers is God's chosen instrument for promoting the Kingdom. This is because the church is meant to embody and testify to the central values of the Kingdom, among which

ONE VOICE

May God...help you live in complete harmony with each other, as is fitting for followers of Christ Jesus. Then all of you can join together with ONE VOICE, giving praise and glory to God, the Father of our Lord Jesus Christ. –Romans 15:5-6 NLT

are oneness, reconciliation, equality, justice, freedom, harmony, peace and love ('shalom'). Furthermore, Christian communicators are conscious of and show respect for God's mysteries. God's ways can never be grasped, let alone be explained. Likewise, the crown of God's creation, people, cannot be fully understood. Christian communicators, therefore, are always aware of their inadequacies when speaking of God, and conscious of 'mystery' when telling the story of God's people.

The communication of Christians is ultimately meant to glorify God. In that sense all Christian communication is an act of worship, a praise of God through the shared word and action of a community living in the consciousness of God's presence. Christian communication is challenged to witness of God's transforming power in all areas of human life.

Paul calls himself and all servants of the Word, "servants of your glory". (Eph 1:12) and thus "servants of your joy"'. (11 Cor. 1:24). The glory of God and the joy of the people should be the hallmark of all Christian communication. These general principles of "Christian" communication will now be elaborated in the context of today's communication problems.

Communication Creates Community

Many people today fear or deplore the loss of community and community spirit. Rather than bringing people together, the mass media often isolates or divides them. Yet communication, including the use of alternative media (such as one-one witnessing), can revitalize communities and rekindle community spirit, because the model for genuine communication, like that for communities of all kinds, is open and inclusive, rather than unidirectional and exclusive.

Genuine communication cannot take place in a climate of division, alienation, isolation, and other barriers which disturb, prevent or distort social interaction. True communication is facilitated when people join together regardless of race, color or religious conviction, and where there is acceptance of and commitment to one another. This is especially true within the Body of Christ, specifically those churches which God has ordained to serve His people in a community. Church ministries must not see themselves as individual silos but interwoven fibers which work together like fishers of men and spread their nets to pull in the lost.

Communication Is Participatory

The mass media have been organized along one-way lines. Their information flows from top to bottom, from the center to the periphery, from the few to the many, from the "information rich" to the "information poor". This has negatively influenced the minds of many people.

There is now a growing awareness that there are information and communication needs, felt by individuals and groups, which the mass media cannot meet. Modern communication technologies could allow a much higher degree of participation than those who control the media systems are willing to grant or to develop. However, communication is, by definition, participatory. It is a two-way process. It is interactive because it shares meaning and establishes and maintains social relationships. The more widespread and powerful the media become, the greater the need for people to engage in their own local or inter-group communication activities. In this way, they will also rediscover and develop traditional forms of communication.

We see in the gospels that Jesus practiced two-way communication. Often he would engage His audience to respond to His words. In Matthew 13:51, Jesus asks His disciples after telling them a parable, "Have you understood all these things?" They responded, "Yes". This was not an isolated example. For Jesus, it was not only important that His listeners hear His Word but respond to it. This was typical of His use of the two-way process.

Communication Liberates

Communication, which liberates, enables people to articulate their own needs and helps them to meet those needs. It enhances their sense of dignity and underlines their ability to fully participate in life.

In addition, we cannot communicate with people whom we regard as inferior, whose basic worth as humans we do not respect. Genuine communication presupposes the recognition that all human beings are of equal worth. The more explicit equality becomes in human interaction, the more easily communication occurs.

There are crude and subtle ways of silencing people. And, at times, Christians are guilty of exercising those methods. It is very easy to justify these actions by simply masking our deeper feelings. We can act outwardly like we are listening, when in reality we have no interest in what someone is saying. We can even respond in a way that implies that we will respond to them at a future date, knowing fully well we do not intend to do so. This type of communication is sinful because it lacks honesty and integrity.

For the Christian, every effort should be made to not only listen but respond to the communicator. Even if it means responding in the negative. Most people can handle a negative response because it is immediate and straightforward. This behavior in itself is liberating not only for the communicator but the listener as well, because the truth has been spoken and the truth will set you free.

Communication is Prophetic

Today's media tries to interpret the signs of the times, because this is part of the public information work to which they are committed. For Christians, the events of the day are part of God's agenda for action. God's plans are revealed in His Word through changing circumstances and new opportunities in our lives. In order to discern and interpret the situation correctly, Christian communicators must listen to God and be led by the Spirit. This is a condition of prophecy. But words are only part of prophecy. They take on real meaning only when they are accompanied by action. Prophetic communication expresses itself in words and deeds. Such prophetic action must be willing to challenge the principalities and powers, and may carry a high price. Prophetic communication serves truth and challenges falsehood. Lies and half-truths are a great threat to communication.

Prophetic communication stimulates critical awareness of the reality constructed by the media and helps people to distinguish truth from falsehood, to discern the subjectivity of the journalist and to disassociate that which is short-lived and trivial from that which is lasting and valuable.

Often it is necessary to develop alternative communication so that prophetic words and deeds can be realized. These alternative forms are manifested in one-on-one public witnessing, Christian published works, and Christian talk shows, to name a few. As the media increases its proliferation of jaded and erroneous biblical truths, the more critical it is for the Christian community to emphasize the importance of sharpening our communication skills.

SUMMARY

"Men of Athens! I see that in every way you are very religious" (Acts 17:22). Paul here is an example of someone being a "perceptive" listener. He heard beyond what the words had to say. He not only heard their words, but also observed their actions, (v. 23). Perceptive listening concentrates on the 93%[5] of non-verbal communication, which makes up the majority of most messages.

In Mark 8:13-21, the Pharisees failed to understand the meaning behind the words, and they were reluctant to ask questions for clarification. Fortunately, Jesus was an excellent communicator. By noticing their confusion, He clarified His message and again asked if they understood what He was trying to convey. For understanding to be complete, the listener must also look beyond words. Again, the non-verbal plays a more significant role the actual words (see the illustration below).

Effective communication is a strong trait of successful leadership. It is not necessary to use lofty words. One simple rule should always be remembered- "Keep It Simple". As Paul was quoted at the beginning of the module,

> *"And when I came to you, brethren, I did not come with superiority of speech or of wisdom, proclaiming to you the testimony of God."*
> *(I Corinthians 2:1 NASB).*

Paul could have easily boasted in his training and experience, however, he knew he had to be all things to all men. Moreover, in order to do that, he needed to always know his audience and communicate accordingly.

By understanding what you think and what feelings you want to express, you can assure that your message will be received successfully. Learn to state "how" you feel when something occurs and then determine "why" you feel this way. When you clarify this for yourself, then your audience can comprehensively understand your message.

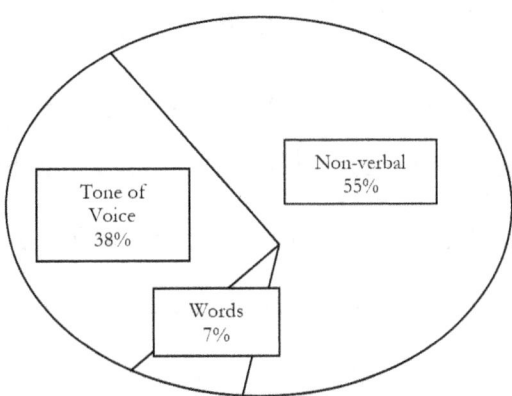

Remember, listening plays a pivotal role in communication. Furthermore, do not overlook the fundamentals of effective communication; speak clearly, listen to the words and the feelings of others; and exchange feedback. All of which contribute to ensuring effective and successful communication.

References:

1. Kenneth O. Gangel, Feeding & Leading: A Practical Handbook on Administration in Churches and Christian Organizations, 1989, Baker Books, Baker Book House Company, Grand Rapids MI, page 213

2. Robert N. Lussier, Management: Concepts, Applications, Skill Development, 1997, South-Western College Publishing, Cincinnati OH, page 324-326

3. Myron Rush, Management: A Biblical Approach, 1983, SP Publications, Victor Books, Wheaton IL, page 122

4. Ibid, pp. 123-126

5. Ibid, page 125

PERSONAL APPLICATION

1. Identify the people closest to you in a working or personal relationship.

2. Identify and list the communication barriers that exist between you and these people.

3. Draft a list of action steps that you can take to minimize these barriers.

4. Read the following article and identify any relevant points in your church-

4 Common Communication Mistakes Churches Make

SmartChurchManagement.com
May 3, 2017

The most important function of communication within an organization/ministry is to inform, persuade and motivate.

Successful organizations/ministries communicate intentionally because they recognize that when leadership fails to communicate effectively, issues arise, conflict presents itself and organizational momentum slows.

We all have different preferences for how we receive information, yet we all crave communication. It is what engages us in our relationships, our employment, and our church.

When staff members (as well as volunteers) understand what, and why, things are happening within the church they feel valued and engaged. However when decisions are made and things go on behind the scenes, which are not communicated, staff members feel dismissed and undervalued.

1. No Communication

In the hustle and bustle of the day, it can be easy to forget that information we are gathering in everything we do should be shared with other people. Oftentimes seemingly insignificant information can have a major impact on another staff member's job.

For example, if church leadership is discussing a new church program, it is their responsibility to think through who will be impacted by this decision and what information needs to be shared before the program is launched. Staff members want to do a good job and can benefit from knowing about initiatives that may impact their job and responsibilities.

2. Controlling Who Receives Information

Sometimes church leaders' control who has access to certain information because it somehow makes them feel more important for knowing something that other people do not.

This hoarding of information can create problems in the workplace. Particularly if staff members are not given the pertinent information needed to do their job.

There is a sensitive balance between sharing enough information to help a staff person move forward on something and sharing confidential information that may not be necessary or applicable.

3. Not Sharing Difficult Information

Sometimes leaders delay sharing information because it is difficult or uncomfortable to talk about. When a church is experiencing challenging times, and major changes are going on, it is even more important to communicate the specifics with staff members.

For example, when church donations are down and difficult budget cuts need to be made, staff members should be made aware of what is going on and what the organization/ministry is doing to address the situation. Staff members who feel like they are part of the problem-solving process feel valued, engaged and can often help identify ways to cut costs or improve operational efficiencies.

4. Poor Communication Process

It is important to establish a predictable process for sharing information. Staff members should know what information is shared, when to expect information to be shared and who the communicator of information will be.

For example, staff members might expect to hear from the senior pastor or business administrator about major church changes, yet their immediate supervisor may share compensation information.

Decision-Making and Problem-Solving

Where is the man who fears the Lord? God will teach him to choose the best. (Psalm 25:12 LB)

As a Christian, the heart of decision-making is knowing God's will. This is the answer to the question, "How does one make the right decisions?" Corporations spend millions of dollars on consultants and data gathering tools to aid them in making decisions. However, a Christian servant-leader's most valuable tool is prayer. It is through prayer that we take the time to seek the Lord's direction and His wisdom. The good news is that God wants to show His people how to make those right decisions.

Decision-making simply put is choosing between alternatives, whereas problem-solving is the process of formulating and implementing a plan of action to eliminate a difficulty.[1]   Problem-solving always involves making decisions, however, just because a decision has been made, doesn't mean the problem has been solved.

Jean Buridan, a fourteenth-century philosopher, spoke often of a certain donkey with high intelligence but a low toleration threshold when it came to making decisions. When placed between two equally attractive bundles of hay, the donkey died of starvation because he could not find a valid reason to choose one over the other.

Because God has a specific plan for each Christian, it is essential that the Lord be included in the decision-making process. To overlook His presence from the initial planning stage to the completion of a task or project, we invite frustration to overshadow every aspect of completing our goals.

KNOWING GOD'S WILL AND DIRECTION

A closer look at the word "will" sheds light on God's perspective. The word "will" has two distinct meanings in the Bible. One definition pertains to a legal declaration of how a person wishes their possessions to be disposed of after their death. However, the definition relevant to this module is explained by Nelson's Illustrated Bible Dictionary below:

- Wishing, desiring, or choosing especially in reference to the will of God. In the gospels, primarily in John, Jesus is said to be acting not according to His own will, but according to the will of the heavenly Father (John 5:30; 6:38). Indeed, doing the will of the Father is Jesus' nourishment (John 4:34), and Jesus does nothing apart from the Father's will (John 5:19). Luke confirms this when he quotes Jesus' statement in the Garden of Gethsemane:

  "Father, if it is Your will, remove this cup from Me, nevertheless not my will, but yours, be done." (Luke 22:42).
  (Nelson's Illustrated Bible Dictionary (Copyright (C) 1986, Thomas Nelson Publishers)

The thrust of Nelson's insight is that, like our Lord Jesus Christ, we must be in communion with the will of the Father. In John 5:19, Jesus provides us with the fundamental principle which is the foundation of sound decision making:

". . . Truly, truly, I say to you, the Son can do nothing of Himself, unless it is something He sees the Father doing; for whatever the Father does, these things the Son also does in like manner."

Intellectually we can acknowledge that we strive to be in harmony with the Father's will. However, sometimes we face a greater hurdle- hearing His counsel. God does not always communicate His will through supernatural means. All too often, the tendency is to seek some supernatural sign or wonder as a confirmation of His communicated will to us. Our pre-occupation with the question, "How can I do what God wants, if he doesn't let me know?" often hides His message from us. This is especially true of those who are intensely task-oriented.

Elijah learned a valuable lesson in looking for the less than spectacular, in seeking the Lord's direction. In I Kings 19:11-12 the scripture tells us,

"Then a great and powerful wind tore the mountains apart and shattered the rocks before the Lord, but the Lord was not in the wind. After the wind, there was an earthquake, but the Lord was not in the earthquake. After the earthquake came the fire, but the Lord was not in the fire. And, after the fire came a gentle whisper."

All too often we don't take the time to listen to that small, still voice that is trying to make its way through the noise of this world.

Myron Rush[2] highlights some points to consider in seeking His will for us:

- *In order to know God's will, you must first be committed to doing it.*

  In Romans 12:1-2, Paul echoes this very point. God does not waste His time communicating His will on people not interested in it. God's will is good, pleasing, and perfect.

- *Recognize God has a specific plan for you, your ministry, organization, or business.*

  "For I know the plans I have for you, declares the Lord, plans to prosper you and not to harm you, plans to give you hope and a future" (Jeremiah 29:11).

"I will instruct you and teach you in the way you should go; I will counsel you and watch over you." (Psalm 32:8).

If we commit ourselves to God, He will communicate His will to us. However, how can we know what He wants of us? Read on.

KNOWING THE BIBLE IS ONE THING KNOWING THE AUTHOR IS ANOTHER

- *God communicates His will by giving us a desire to do what He wants done.*

    God promises to put His will in us and then give us the power or resources to accomplish it. This is demonstrated in Philippians 2:13, "For it is God who works in you to will and to act according to His good purpose".

    All too often, His will begins as a desire in our hearts. It is from this desire that His will begins to grow and eventually He confirms that initial spark, which began as a simple desire. Remember God's promise, *"Delight yourself in the Lord, and He will give us the desires of our heart"*, (Psalm 37:4). Therefore, start examining your heart for His will.

- *If the desire is God's will, we will have a peace about doing it and the power to achieve it.*

    Be aware that He did not say He would give us *every* desire of our hearts! The promise is conditional. If we are totally committed to God and His will for us, then God will give us the desires of our heart, because He put them there. Paul points this out in Philippians 2:13.

Moreover, take note, where God leads, He provides. If the power and resources are not materializing, then examine your heart and listen for that small, still voice.

THE ESSENTIALS OF DECISION MAKING

The following prerequisite questions for sound decision-making, should be answered before beginning with the decision-making process.[3]

1. Am I committed to doing God's will in this situation? (Romans 12:1-2)

2. Are the desires of my heart to pursue this particular course? (Psalm 37:4)

3. Does God provide the power and resources to accomplish this desire? (Philippians 2:13)

4. Does God give me peace to continue working on the project and to make the necessary decisions to achieve it? (Isaiah 26:3)

If you can answer "yes" to all the questions, then you can proceed confidently with making the decisions you need to make.

After confirming your progress to move forward, the following essentials serve as guidelines to comprehensive decision-making:

- *Correctly diagnose the issue or the problem*

    Wrong decisions are often made on false assumptions and incorrect diagnoses. In the thirteenth chapter of the book of Numbers, some of the spies returned to Moses with a wrong assessment of the situation. Had their misinterpretation not been contradicted, it may have cost the nation of Israel the continuation of its people.

- *Gather and analyze the facts*

    Consider the following fact-gathering questions as an aid in the decision-making process:

    1. What are the conditions and circumstances surrounding this situation? (Proverbs 24:3-4)

    2. What does the Bible say about this issue or situation? (Joshua 1:8)

    3. What is the Lord telling me in my prayer over this matter? (Jeremiah 33:3)

    4. What counsel do I get from people in this situation? (Proverbs 11:14)

    5. What are my interests and desires in this situation? (Psalm 37:4)

- *Develop alternatives*

    Never make important decisions until other alternatives are considered or formulated. This ensures choosing against the first possible solution. Thinking through several alternative, forces the decision maker to consider all the facts and data carefully. It also avoids quick and error riddled decisions. Read Proverbs 19:2.

- *Evaluate the pros and cons of the alternatives chosen*

  Study the strengths and weaknesses of the probable alternatives to eliminate the least plausible alternatives. Read Luke 14:31-32.

- *Select from among the positive alternatives*

  Selecting from among the positive alternatives may not be as easy as it appears. The reason being is that at this point, a decision must be made. The subversive actions that can creep in are procrastination or the "paralysis of analysis". These actions can easily delay a decision or even cause a missed opportunity. Read Psalm 32:8

COLLABROTIVE DECISION-MAKING

In the book of Acts, we have two examples of collaborative decision making in the early church. The apostles utilized two different approaches in dealing with the two challenges they faced. In both approaches, one thing is clear, the church leaders took the lead and spearheaded the efforts that were necessary to solve the problems.

Upon closer review, we see that the congregation in both instances was a part of the decision-making process. The goal of church leadership and the congregation should always be to speak and act as one united body. Both the leaders and the church body should pray and work together to achieve unity of mind.

Open communication between leadership and those they serve provide a defense shield against obstacles such as complacency, pride, power-building, and self-serving interests. This is especially true when the church body is involved. When appropriate, including the church body it promotes a healthy family environment.

In the sixth chapter of Acts, conflicts between two groups of believers within the church provided an opportunity to work together. The issue was over a fair distribution of provisions between the Hebrew and Hellenistic Christians. The apostles wasted no time in formulating a plan to address the issue. Once they assessed the problem and designed an approach to remedy the problem, they presented it to the body. Their plan met with approval among the congregation and, it was put into practice.

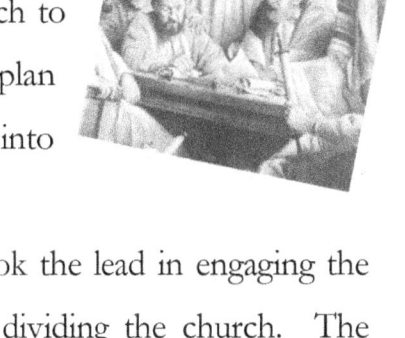

In the fifteenth chapter of Acts, again the apostles took the lead in engaging the whole church in discussing the controversy which was dividing the church. The leadership allowed open discussion and debate, revealing opposing views. However, the final decision to resolve the issue was reserved for the apostles, through the power of the Holy Spirit.

Kenneth O. Gangel[4] points out that there is no magic to effective team decision-making. He states that it takes time to develop a leadership team. He also offers some key points to remember:

- Each member has one voice – meaning each member *only* has one voice and one person should not dominate. On the other hand, each member has *at least one voice* and everyone needs to be actively involved.

- Each member has a responsibility to express his or her opinion. Everyone should express it when the discussion is being conducted. Not a week later, in the parking lot, in a whisper to the person next to him, etc.

- Each member must listen respectfully to all other opinions. This kind of posture takes maturity. We cannot be a respecter of persons and place more emphasis on one person over another because of their station in life, economic background, where they live, etc. God gives each one of us wisdom.

- Each member must detach himself emotionally from his own ideas. The stronger the link between someone's attitude and the ownership of material and non-material things, the greater one's immaturity is demonstrated. The mature person can suggest an idea, "place it on the table", and deliberately allow his fellow decision-makers to weigh it, evaluate it, attack it, build on it, or take a different direction.

- Each member must publicly support the group's decision – A consensus means that the group has agreed in principal to do something, and they now stand united in the decision. A consensus does not mean absolute unanimity. It does mean it is a decision that you can support.

- Each member must keep group processes confidential. Whatever discussions, disagreements or ideas are no one's business outside of the group. Everyone involved must have the confidence that they can express their opinions and thoughts without them going beyond the group. Especially when anything can be misconstrued or taken out of context.

Scripture does not disclose specific detail, guidelines, steps, or rules for problem-solving and decision-making. What we do find are general principles, which can be applied. Additionally, there can be no mistake regarding the outcome of all decisions- a unified body. Paul writes in Philippians 2:2 –

> **"Make my joy complete by being of the same mind, maintaining the same love, united in spirit, intent on one purpose."**

THE PROBLEM-SOLVING PROCESS

With a fundamental understanding of decision-making, problem solving becomes less intimidating. However, it is important to distinguish a "problem" from a "condition". Conditions are generally uncontrollable circumstances or situations beyond our control. If this distinction is misdiagnosed, frustration, confusion, and discouragement will set in.

For example, your car transmission breaks down on the way to work. The *condition* is the transmission breakdown. However, this condition now may spawn a variety of *problems*, such as- Do I tow it home or to a mechanic shop? How will I pay for the repair? How will I get to work while the car is in the shop? Learning to identify the conditions from the problems will reduce misdirected energy.

We can make the problem-solving process as complicated or simple as we choose. The illustrations below will identify which process your mind maps to immediately when faced with a problem. There is no right or wrong approach, it's just a matter of preference.

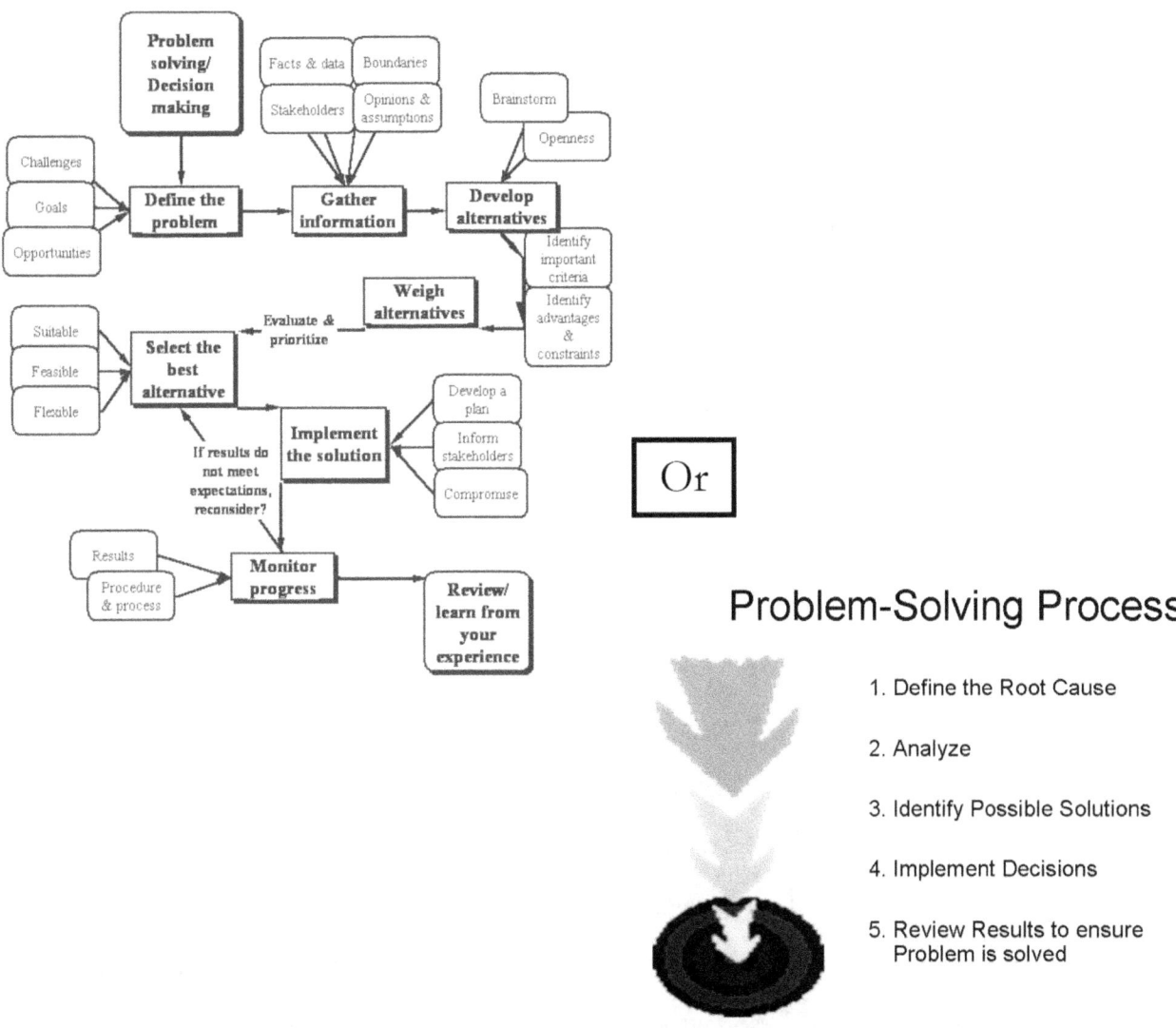

Problem-Solving Process

1. Define the Root Cause

2. Analyze

3. Identify Possible Solutions

4. Implement Decisions

5. Review Results to ensure Problem is solved

SUMMARY

The following are universal principals of problem solving:

- Determine if the situation is a problem or condition.

  If it is a condition, identify the problems that was created by the condition. Do not expect to change the condition.

- Clearly state the problem.

  False assumptions produce wrong outcomes. A problem cannot be solved if it is not properly defined.

- Determine what will be gained or lost in solving the problem.

  Will solving the problem cause a bigger problem? Weigh the gains and pains!

- Identify alternative methods and solutions.

  Many times, there is more than one solution to a problem. When possible, involve those affected by the problem for further insight.

- Identify the cost of each alternative.

  Money is not the only consideration. Consider the cost of time, labor, and resources.

- Choose between alternatives

  Sometimes finding a solution involves some give and take. Allow an open mind to prevail in finding a solution.

- Delegate action steps and begin implementation.

  Be ready to implement actions to bring about change

- Evaluate the progress.

  Many times, a solution looks good on paper, however, over time it does not play out as it was intended. Close monitoring after actions are implemented will allow for correction, revision, or an early return to the drawing board.

There are three factors[5] which are apparent in the success or failure of decisions. A healthy attitude towards these factors will go a long way in dealing with the results.

1. *The element of risk.* There is no way to know in advance the results of a decision. Every decision contains a certain element of risk. The question becomes, "What is the tolerance level of an adverse decision?" How much risk can the principals that are involved tolerate? The worse case scenario should always be evaluated and weighted before pressing forward.

2. *The consequences of failure* – Do not dwell on the consequences of failure. Accept the possibility of failure, but do not dwell on it. Count it as a cost and prepare for it whenever possible. Do not allow the fear of failure to overwhelm the will of God.

3. *The rewards of success* – Success is never assured. Allow success to serve as motivation in accomplishing the Lord's plan. Approach everything that is done, with confidence knowing that it is not the self who empowers, but the power of the Holy Spirit.

There are times when we want to embrace what Charlie Brown sighed in one of his comic strips, "There's no problem so big that I can't run from it." We all have been there. John C. Maxell[6] makes this observation, ". . . I have noticed that the size of the person is more important than the size of the problem. Problems look larger or smaller according to whether the person is large or small."

Problems never stop coming. In fact, problems give meaning to our life. The challenges that we encounter most often build our character in a way that would not have happened without the challenge. More importantly, we learn to have a greater dependency on God. When we get to a place when we no longer feel we need His help, we begin to set ourselves up as little "gods". As we mature in Christ, we increase our understanding that He is the one who enables us.

When the challenges that occur in our lives become our primary focus, we lose sight of the problem solver – Jesus Christ. Remember when Peter stepped out of that boat as he walked on the water towards the Lord. He soon began to sink not because he could not complete the journey, but because he took his focus off the Lord!

We too need to be mindful of this same principal. Like Peter, we have unique abilities, talents, training and so forth, but all of that is rendered useless when we focus only on the problem. Develop your problem-solving techniques and principles so that the Lord can enable you through His Holy Spirit to overcome life's challenges.

Additionally, as you develop others around you, John C. Maxell[7] provides some effective suggestions for coaching them:

- Never allow others to think you always have the best answers. This will only make them dependent on you.

- Ask questions. Provoke people to think through the entire process of their problem and its possible resolution.

- Become a coach, not a king. A coach brings out the best in others, helping them to reach deep down inside and discover their potential. A king only gives commands.

- List their solutions on paper. Integrate your ideas with theirs until they have ownership of them

- Move towards a resolution. Ask them to decide on the best solution to their problem.

- Develop a game plan.

- Ask them to take ownership and responsibility for the game plan. Let them set up a time frame and accountability process.

References:

1. Management: A Biblical Approach, Myron Rush, Victor Books, 1985, page 108

2. Ibid, pages 100-102

3. Ibid, page 102

4. Feeding and Leading, Kenneth O. Gangel, Baker Books, 1989, pages 195-198

5. Op Cit, Management: A Biblical Approach, page 107

6. Developing the Leader Within You, John C. Maxwell, Thomas Nelson, Inc, 1993, page 82

7. Ibid, page 95

PERSONAL APPLICATION

1. In what ways can you detach yourself emotionally from your ideas? Make a list.

2. Identify one or two issues in your life that are challenging you.

3. Apply the decision-making or problem solving steps and write a short narrative on the results.

4. Apply the team decision-making principles in a meeting at work or ministry and write a short narrative on the results.

Time Management

There is an appointed time for everything. And there is a time for every event under heaven- (Ecclesiastes 3:1, NAS)

Y**our Church** magazine conducted a nationwide survey of pastors and discovered that, if they could—

- 61% of the pastors would spend less time in meetings
- 37% of the pastors would spend less time mediating conflict
- 34% of the pastors would spend less time counseling

If they could redirect that time, they would spend it in –

- Evangelism (58%)
- Personal devotions (66%)
- Sermon preparation (73%)
- Prayer (75%)[1]

In the same research, John LaRue, Jr.[1], discovered that pastors who were most satisfied about their use of time had a better perspective, than those pastors who were less satisfied with their use of time. The most satisfied pastors shared the following, they –

- Limited their work to less than the average of fifty-five hours per week (workweek ranges fell between forty-five and fifty-five hours)
- Learned to accept the fact that the job will never be finished

- Regularly take a least one full day off every week
- Used all of their vacation time (twenty-five days a year on average)

Sound time management principles enable people to get more done in less time with better results. Therefore, in order to optimize your time, it is essential that you determine the things that are important to you, and then when you identify them, prioritize them. By doing so, misguided activities will not rob a leader of one of the most vital resources- time.

Many people do not use their time effectively, because they are not taught how to use their time effectively.[2]   As a result, companies like Franklin Quest earn over $35 million dollars a year from time management seminars and materials[3]. Regrettably, many people do not regularly practice the time management skills they learn.

WORK, LEISURE AND BALANCE OF TIME

"There are people who go on indefinitely preparing for life instead of living it", Paul Tournier points out in his book, "The Adventure of Living"[4]. Especially in ministry, work should not be done for gain, but for the love of doing it. The labor we do for the Lord should be a passion which drives us to accomplish things beyond our abilities.

Unfortunately, most people do not like their work. It is through this negative attitude that complacency, apathy, and dissatisfaction often spill over onto ministry service. As a result, the people around them, many times, are exposed to their disenchantment, thereby causing them to wane in their enthusiasm which causes the ministry to suffer.

So, "Why work?" Simply put, it's biblical! We first see God's instruction for us in Genesis, "The Lord took the man and put him into the Garden of Eden to cultivate it and keep it". (Genesis 2:15) The Lord ordained before the curse that work was of value to our lives and of service to Him. Conversely, work took on a different perspective after the fall, as we see in Genesis 3:17-19.

More specifically, in Exodus 34:21, God gave this command . . . "You shall work six days", to the Old Testament believer. Paul underscores this in II Thessalonians 3:10, by stating, "If anyone will not work, neither let him eat."

One of the primary purposes of work is to develop the character of the worker. While the carpenter is building a house, the house is building the carpenter. His skill, diligence, manual dexterity and judgment are refined. A job is not merely a task designed to earn money; it is also intended to produce godly character in the life of the worker.[5]

Dorothy Sayers points out, "The first [proposition], stated quite briefly, is that work is not, primarily, a thing one does to live, but the thing one lives to do. It is, or it should be, the full expression of the worker's faculties, the thing in which he finds spiritual, mental and bodily satisfaction, and the medium in which he offers himself to God."[6]

The work we do, outside or inside of ministry, should never be associated with laziness or mediocrity. Otherwise, those watchful eyes around us will draw a parallel with those attributes and God. We should do everything with the highest standards, which are worthy of our Lord.

> *Whatever your hand finds to do, do it with all your might; . . ." Proverbs 9:10*
>
> *. . . but the precious possession of a man is diligence. Proverbs 12:27*
>
> *. . . but with our labor and hardship we kept working night and day so that we would not be a burden to any of you; . . . as a model for you, so that you would follow our example. II Thessalonians 3:8-9*

A BALANCED WORK LIFE

Working hard must be balanced with our other priorities in life. All work and no play, etc. It is important to note that our first priority is our relationship with the Lord. "But seek first His kingdom and His righteousness" (Matthew 6:33). The second priority is our family.

By allowing your work life to consume your time, especially if you have difficulty

managing it, it will compromise your walk in the Lord. Take precautions to guard yourself and avoid turning into a "workaholic". By concentrating on making the most of your work time you ensure accomplishing more with less time. Remember, the Lord worked six days, but rested on the seventh. He instilled this example for our physical, mental and spiritual well-being.

The graphic illustration on the next page depicts the ideal place to be as it relates to our work life. The ideal place to be is between these extremes- "Laziness" and a "Compulsive Work Behavior". A healthy balanced life that involves our relationship with God, our family and ourselves reflect this balance. The fulcrum in this illustration is our commitment to God.

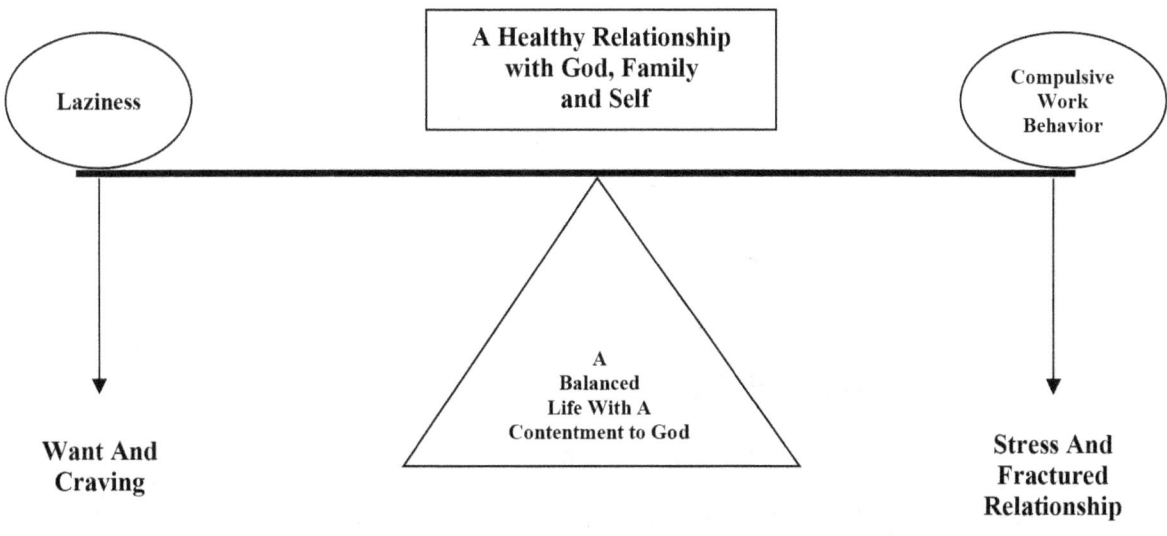

TOOLS OF THE TRADE

Analyze Your Time

People do not often realize how much time is wasted until they sit down and take a hard look at their use of time. Jennifer Labbs[7] points out that managers on average wasted about 15 minutes on hold on the phone, which adds up to two weeks per year per person[8]. Being cognizant of time stealers allows you to plan other activities during these non-productive periods such as read your mail while on hold. Take the time to analyze your use of time and look for areas to better manage your time. This is also a great opportunity to break bad habits.

 Time Saver Tool: Time Log[8]

Set up a time log to track your daily activities to visually illustrate how your time is spent. Track your time every day for one to two weeks. Set up 15 minutes time slots to record what you did. See the following time log example below:

Daily Time Log For - Day: _____ Date: _____	
8:00 a.m.	
8:15 a.m.	
8:30 a.m.	
8:45 a.m.	
9:00 a.m.	
9:15 a.m.	

Analyze the daily time logs. Review your notes, then label them with codes to identify the activities. For example-

HP – Time spent on high priority activities

LP – Time spent on low priority activities

TM – Areas you spent too much time

TL – Areas you spent too little time

D – Areas you could have delegated activities

B – Areas that your boss controls

E – Areas that your employees or co-workers control

C –   Crisis situations

Review your notes every few days and look for reoccurring time waster activities. Determine how much time you are spending in certain areas, look for patterns

Draft and Follow a Time Management System

Four key components are needed in a time management system

- Priorities – Learn to set priorities. Knowing what action items need more attention than low priority items aid in concentrating on the essentials of the day.

- Objectives – Learn to develop goals. Set daily and weekly objectives to accomplish and review your accomplishments at the end of the week.

- Plans – Develop strategic operating plans to complete your objectives.

- Schedules – Use a planning sheet, such as GNATT or PERT charts. They are excellent tools to schedule your time. Schedule each week in advance.

① **Time Saver Tool:** Apply the Three-step Method

Step 1:   Plan Each Week

At the end of each week plan the upcoming week. Review your past week and use the information to aid you in setting up the new week of activities. Begin with listing the goals you want to complete by the end of the week.

After setting your goals, set reasonable objectives to accomplish your goals. The ability to distinguish between the two enables you to manage your time more efficiently. To monitor your progress, check-off your objectives as you complete them. This will aid you in visualizing the completion of your goals.

Step 2:   Schedule Each Week

Scheduling your work helps in organizing your work for the week[9]. Draft a weekly template to visualize your activities for the week. Start your scheduling by filling in uncontrollable time slots such as meetings or appointments. Be flexible with your time. One key to time management is to not prioritize your schedule, but to schedule your priorities weekly and daily.[10]

Step 3:   Schedule Each Day

At the end of the day schedule the next day. Base your next day's objectives on your plan for the week. Again, begin by scheduling activities you have no control over. Leave your daily schedule flexible.

Scheduling tips:

- Don't be too optimistic. Schedule ample time between activities.

- Once you have prioritized your tasks, focus whenever possible on only one task at a time. Peter Drucker points out that few people seem to do an incredible number of things.[11]

- Schedule high-priority items during "prime time", at the peak of your day when you perform at your best.

- Try to schedule time for unexpected events.

- Do not perform an unscheduled task before determining its priority.

☼ **Time Saver Tool:** Pray for Your Plans

Martin Luther once said that he had so much to do on a particular day, that it was necessary for him pray for at least four hours[12]. This may not go over well in today's fast-paced society, but the point is still the same. We need to take time to seek the Lord's direction each day for His plan in our lives.

We can incorporate prayer in a number of ways:

- Pray over your to-do list every morning

- Pray for new ideas or to recognized unnoticed problems

- Pray with family, friends, or associates over goals

ⓘ **Time Saver Tool:** Fill Up Your Calendar with the "Right Stuff"!

A crammed calendar can be a blessing or a curse. What matters most is what it is filled with and in what priority. If we have our priorities in order, our calendar will contain these priorities:

- *Time with God.* The time we dedicate to worship, pray, meditate and read His Word.

- *Time with our Family.* The time we invest in our family and the time they invest in us. Your calendar should show time with your spouse, children, family, friends, and leisure.

- *Time for You.* Set time aside for you to open up the relief valve from pressures. Schedule time for recreation or time just doing nothing but relaxing.

- *Time for Fellowship with the Body of Christ.* Do not overlook those times when you gather with other believers and you share your common faith in Him. Spend time in small home groups, prayer groups, or just gather and break bread.

- *Time for Other People.* Allow for unplanned time for working with other people for their goals. Do not utilize this time for counseling, but as a time for working with others to achieve their goals.

- *Time to Plan.* Review your progress against your goals. Make time to plan and review each day, each week and each month. Use this time to share your calendar with your spouse and family for a proper perspective.

References

1. John c. LaRue, Jr., "Time Management for Hard Working Pastors", "Your Church", (November/December 1998), page 80.

2. Gene Levine, "Finding Time", Bobbin (June 1994), Vol. 35, Issue 10, pp. 113-114.

3. Amy Feldman, "We'll Make You Scary", Forbes, February 14, 1994, p. 96.

4. Paul Tournier, "The Adventure of Living", Harper & Row, New York, 1965.

5. Crown Ministries: Small Group Study, Crown Ministries, Inc., 1986, pp. 96-97.

6. Dorothy L. Sayers, "Creed or Chaos?", Methuen and Company, Ltd., London, 1954.

7. Jennifer Laabs, "Executives on Hold", Personnel Journal (January 1994), Vol. II, Iss. 1, pp.18-20.

8. Robert N. Lussier, PH.D., Management-Concepts, Applications, Skill Development, South-west College Publishing, 1997, pp. 190-191.

9. Stephen Covey, "First Things First", Success (April 1994), Vol. 41, Iss. 3, pp. 8a-8d.

10. Ibid

11. Gene Levine, "Finding Time", Bobbin (June 1994), Vol. 35, Iss. 10, pp. 113-114.

12. Edward R. Dayton, "Tools for Time Management", Zondevan Publishing House, 1983, Grand Rapids, Michigan, p. 148.

SUMMARY

For Christian leaders, God's timing plays a major role in their life. Scripture points out that He has His own schedule. Our Lord Jesus recognized His activities and decisions were always in harmony with His Father's plan.

Will Rogers used to say, "It's not so much what you do each day, it's what you get done that counts." Paul the apostle, emphasized this same point by writing, "Therefore be careful how you walk, not as unwise men but as wise, making the most of your time, because the days are evil." Ephesians 5:15-16. Therefore, be wise with your time and seek God's guidance in whatever you plan. But, never forget, we only have the moment, the future is His!

What is your time worth?

The table below shows you what your time is worth by the hour and by the minute based on 244 eight-hour working days per year (assuming a five-day work week less vacation and holidays):

IF YOUR ANNUAL EARNINGS ARE:	EVERY HOUR IS WORTH (ROUNDED TO $):	EACH MINUTE IS WORTH:
$10,000	$5.00	$.09
$15,000	$8.00	$.13
$20,000	$10.00	$.17
$25,000	$13.00	$.21
$30,000	$15.00	$.26
$35,000	$18.00	$.30
$40,000	$20.00	$.34
$50,000	$26.00	$.43
$60,000	$31.00	$.51
$75,000	$39.00	$.64
$100,000	$51.00	$.85

PERSONAL APPLICATION

1. Fill out the time log provided and track your activities for a week. Afterwards, do the following-

   - Write an evaluation of your findings. Make notes on the log and identify the time stealers

   - Set goals for improvements. Look over your time log and determine areas you could target for improvement. Then, start the process over again with a new list.

2. Concurrently with the exercise above, fill out the Activity Rank worksheet. Follow the directions on the worksheet and use it in conjunction with the time log exercise above.

3. Coach someone within your ministry or someone you know and help them to organize their time and activities.

Conflict Management

What is the source of quarrels and conflicts among you? Is not the source your pleasures that wage war in your members? James 4:1

Conflict exists whenever *people are in disagreement and opposition.*[1] Unfortunately, the Church is not immune to conflict. Although, in some cases, conflict can serve a good purpose by distinguishing those who are faithful. We see this example in I Corinthians 11:17-19. As a result, constructive conflict management can sometimes prove to be one of the most important skills a leader can aquire.[2]

The word "conflict" comes the Latin *fligere*, meaning literally "strike together." Whenever one person's needs collide with the needs of another person, conflicts can arise. If people had no desire to strive, to fulfill goals and aspirations, conflicts would almost be nonexistent.

Conflict can also be defined as *"open and hostile opposition occurring as a result of differing vienpoints."*[3] However, conflict is distinctly different from disagreement. People can disagree without hostility being involved. On the other hand, conflict always involves hostility to some degree.

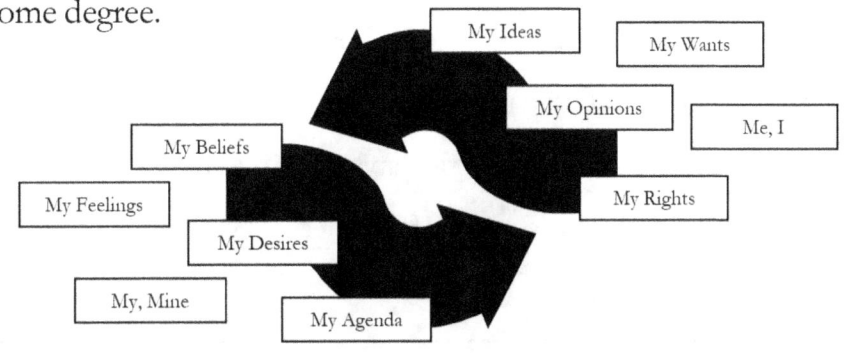

My Ideas   My Wants   My Opinions   Me, I   My Beliefs   My Rights   My Feelings   My Desires   My, Mine   My Agenda

Conflict comes from our own selfish desires and passions – James 4:1

111

The core of the sources of conflict lie in man's original sin, our own agenda, rather than God's. In James 4:1-6, he is explicit about how our self-centered, selfish desire and passions open the door for conflict. In addition, Proverbs points out that "pride only breeds quarrels" (Proverbs 13:10). For this reason, it is no wonder that conflict continues today.

In a situation where conflict occurs, the objective is always to impose our own beliefs, ideas, agendas or opinions on others. We tend to draw a narrow bead on ourselves as we draw attention and promote ourselves by convincing others of our position.

In their book *Church Fights*[4], Speed Leas and Paul Kittlaus point out three ways in which conflict is experienced:

- *Intrapersonal conflict*: The contest one has when different parts of the self-compete with one another. Example, "I want to be a beloved pastor, but I also want to be a preacher who speaks the truth."

- *Interpersonal conflict*: Personality differences that are not related primarily to issues. Example; "I like to think of myself as a strong, independent person, but my administrative board chairperson treats me like an incompetent who must be told what to do."

- *Substantive conflict*: Disputes over facts, values, goals and beliefs. Example: "I think we ought to put a new roof on the church, but the social concerns committee wants to open a clothes closet for the poor."

CONFLICT MANAGEMENT STYLES

On the next page, five conflict management styles have been identified in dealing with conflict. The five styles are based on two dimensions of concerns- concern for others' needs and concern for our own needs.[5]

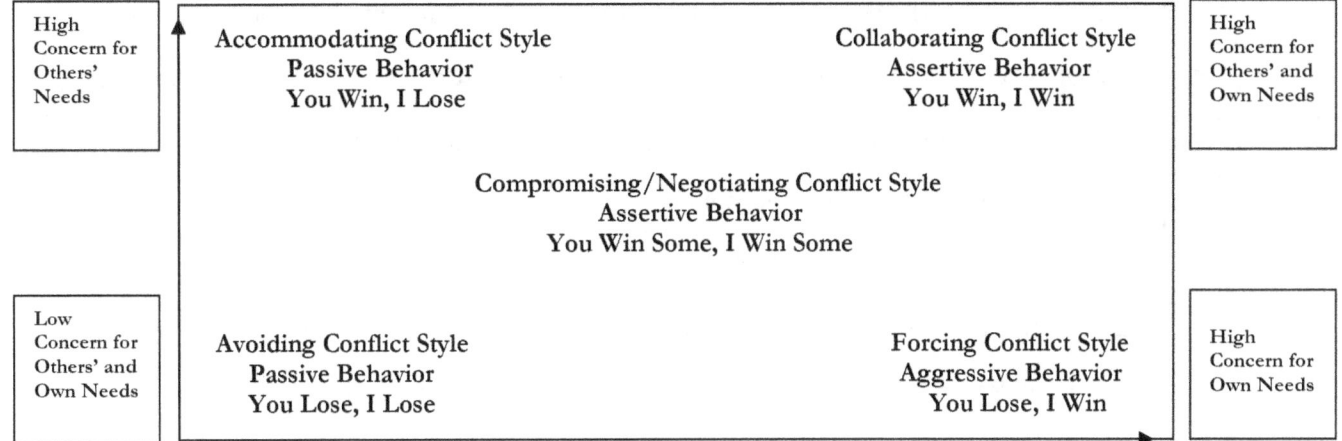

Avoiding Conflict Style:

The ***avoiding conflict*** style user attempts to passively ignore the conflict rather than resolve it. When you avoid conflict, you are being unassertive and uncooperative. A "lose-lose" situation can be created because the conflict is not resolved.

The advantage to this style is that it may maintain relationships that would be hurt through conflict resolution. The disadvantage is the fact that conflicts do not get resolved.

Appropriate use for this style is when:

1. Conflict is trivial
2. Your stake in the issue is not high
3. Confrontation will damage an important relationship
4. You don't have time to resolve the conflict
5. Emotions are high

Accommodating Conflict Style:

The ***accommodating conflict*** style user attempts to resolve conflict by passively giving in to the other party. When you use this style, you are being unassertive but cooperative. A "win-lose" situation is created because you satisfy someone else's needs and neglect your own.

The advantage of this style is that relationships are maintained by doing things the other person's way. The disadvantage is that it is counterproductive. The overuse of this style can result in people taking advantage of the accommodator.

Appropriate use for this style is when:

1. The person enjoys being a follower
2. Maintaining relationships outweighs all other considerations
3. The changes agreed to are not important to the accommodator
4. The time to resolve the conflict is limited

Forcing Conflict Style:

The *forcing conflict style* attempts to resolve the conflict by using aggressive behavior to get your way. When this style is used, the behavior is uncooperative and aggressive. The user does whatever it takes to satisfy his or her own needs at the expense of others. A "win-lose" situation is created.

The advantage to this style is that better organizational decisions, rather than less effective, compromised, decisions will be made when the aggressor is correct. The disadvantage is that overuse to this style leads to hostility and resentment toward the user.

Appropriate use for this style is when:

1. Unpopular action must be taken on important issues
2. Commitment by others to the proposed action is not crucial to its implementation
3. Maintaining relationships is not critical
4. The conflict resolution is urgent

Compromising/Negotiating Conflict Style:

The *negotiating conflict style* attempts to resolve the conflict through assertive give-and-take concessions. This style uses moderate assertiveness and cooperation. A "I-win partly, I-lose partly" situation is created through compromise.

The advantage to this style is that conflict is resolved quickly and working relationships are maintained. The disadvantage to this style is that comprise may lead to counterproductive results. Overuse of this style leads to people playing games, such as asking for twice as much as they need.

Appropriate use for this style is when:

1. Unpopular action must be taken on important issues

2. Commitment by others to a proposed action is not crucial to its implementation

3. Maintaining relationships is not critical

4. Conflict resolution is urgent

Collaborating Conflict Style:

The *collaborating conflict style* assertively attempts to jointly resolve the conflict with the best solution agreeable to all parties. It also called the "problem-solving" style. The user is both assertive and cooperative. This style is based on open and honest communication. This style truly creates a "win-win" situation.

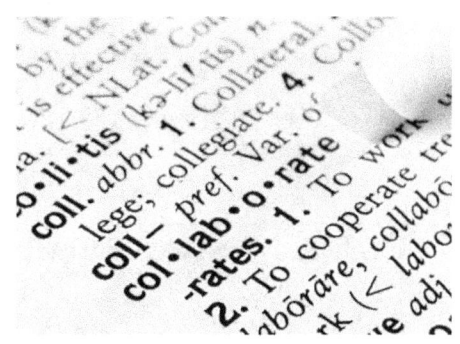

The advantage to this style tends to lead to the best solution to the conflict using assertive behavior. The disadvantage is that the skill, effort, and time it takes to resolve the conflict is usually greater and longer than with the other styles.

Appropriate use for this style is when:

1. You are dealing with an important issue that requires an optimal solution

2. People are willing to place the group goal before self-interest

3. Maintaining relationships is important

4. Time is available

5. A peer conflict exists

POSITIVE ASPECTS OF DISAGREEMENTS

- Disagreements can lead to individual and/or organizational growth. "As iron sharpens iron, so one man sharpens another" (Proverbs 27:17)

- Disagreement can reveal a need for change. The seasoned leader welcomes disagreement because it forces him to evaluate his own position and possibly make positive changes where needed. Read Proverbs 18:15

- Disagreement can help a leader become more tolerate of opposing views. It is important that a leader temper his reactions to opposing viewpoints. Learn to "agree to disagree". The leader also learns to accept criticism as a growth tool. Read Proverbs 23:12

> Good leadership requires you to surround yourself with **people** of diverse perspectives who can disagree with you without fear of retaliation.
>
> *Doris Kearns Goodwin*

FOUR BASIC APPORACHES IN DEALING WITH CONFLICT

Below are four typical approaches in which people deal with conflict. Can you find your style?

1. Attempt to avoid conflict by retreating from it

2. Attempt to avoid conflict by circumventing the major issues and focusing on minor points

3. Attempt to avoid conflict by dealing with side issues

4. Identifying the real issues of conflict and working our way through them to a satisfactory resolution

SCRIPTUAL POINTS TO HANDLING CONFRONTATON

First, make sure you are dealing with the facts. No guesses or hearsay will suffice. Deuteronomy 19:15 states never to convict anyone with only the testimony of one person. Two or more witnesses is best.

Second, always make the initial confrontation in private between you and the person involved. Proverbs 25:9-10 tell us that this is a good method to avoid slander. Avoid making a problem a public issue. Resolve conflict privately whenever possible. Public conflict only compounds the problem and undermines people's trust.

Third, when working to resolve conflict and the other person involved is uncooperative, ask a third party to join you and try again. This principle is stated in Matthew 18:16. Involve others only after you are thoroughly convinced that they need to get involved. This step provides a neutral party and gives evidence that a sincere effort to resolve the problem is being made.

Fourth, if the person continues to resist resolving the conflict, you may need to dissolve the relationship. Matthew 18:17 allows for this principle if every effort has been exhausted to resolve the issue. However, always leave the door open for repentance and forgiveness, as illustrated in Luke 17:3.

HANDLING EXPECTATIONS: DECIDING HOW TO RESPOND[2]

- *Know yourself.* Strip away the expectations others have placed on you and know the answers to these self-examination questions. Who am I? What can I do? With am I struggling with? What are my strengths and weaknesses?

- *Be transparent.* Leaders cannot do it all. If certain areas of ministry seem overwhelming, do not hesitate to ask the Lord to provide help through others or by improving your own skills. Seek other church leaders to help you by freeing you up to concentrate on your strengths.

- *Be inner directed.* The inner-directed person derives values, motivation, and purpose from within, as the Lord has blessed. Avoid feedback from problem people. Remember that if God has called us, he will equip us, work within us and direct our work.

- *Be purposeful in pursuing your course.* Constantly remind yourself and those you lead of your commitment and vision.

- *Be prepared to absorb some misunderstanding.* Leadership is the ability to absorb pain. Realize that everyone may not love you and they may even misunderstand your purest motives. Concentrate on meeting God's expectations of you first, above all else.

References:

1. Management: Concepts, Applications and Skills Development, South-Western College Publishing, 1997, page 463.

2. "Nordstrom: Respond to Unreasonable Customer Requests!", Planning Review (May/June, 1994), Vol. 22, Iss. 3, pp. 17-18.

3. Myron Rush, "Management: A Biblical Approach", Victor Books Publishing, 1985, Wheaton, Ill, p. 202.

4. Leas, S. and P. Kittlaus. 1973. Church fights: Managing conflict in the local church. Philadelphia, Westminster.

5. Op cit., Management: Concepts, Applications and Skills Development, p. 464.

6. Op cit., Management: A Biblical Approach, pp. 206-207

7. Leadership Handbook of Management and Administration, Christianity Today, Inc. and Baker Book House, Grand Rapids, Michigan, pp.192-193.

SUMMARY

It would be unrealistic to think that we can avoid conflict if we just try hard enough. What is realistic is that a leader, through preparation and the enabling of the Holy Spirit, can work through challenges when they arise.

Conflict is not always disruptive or destructive. Opposing viewpoints and disagreements can sometimes flush out issues, which can only be resolved by discussing them openly. How many times have you sat in a meeting and avoided the 800-pound gorilla in the room? The gorilla being that issue which everyone has tried vigorously to avoid for fear that it would cause dissention.

Understanding the issue is critical to achieving resolution. Learning to drill down to the core of an issue will circumvent misdirected energy. Too often, the symptoms are treated, and the cause is overlooked. But, like any competent medical professional, the key is to probe and analyze until the real issue is discovered.

Every conflict or issue is unique. Therefore, no one's conflict management style is always best. Learning the characteristics of each style will enable you to apply the best approach for the situation. Everyone has a preferred style, but learning to be fluid allows the negotiator to move seamlessly between styles.

Remember, challenges can be opportunities. When challenges are avoided or ignored, opportunities can be lost. Imagine Jesus or Paul turning from the issues that confronted them constantly. Jesus dealt with the Pharisees directly. Sometimes mildly. But He never failed to resolve an issue before moving on to the next challenge. As for Paul, he was a tremendous model of successful conflict management by not shrinking from a challenge. He never pretended to be a superhero, but he always equipped himself with the full armor of God!

PERSONAL APPLICAITON

1. Identify your preferred conflict management style and explain why you prefer it.

2. Identify which conflict management style you like the least and explain why.

3. Identify one or two areas of conflict at work, in your ministry or in your life.

4. Analyze the issue(s) and develop possible solution(s), which can bring reconciliation as soon as possible.

Module 9

Servant-Leadership

Then I heard the voice of the Lord saying, "Whom shall I send and who will go for Us? Then I said, "Here am I. Send me!" Isaiah 6:8

In search of Leadership- this is our quest. A stark reality within the Church today is that, "Leadership remains one of the glaring needs of the church", according to George Barna, a church expert and statistician[1]. Barna later wrote some sobering conclusions based on his research:

"After fifteen years of digging into the world around me, I have reached several conclusions regarding the future of the Christian church in America. The central conclusion is that the American church is dying due to lack of strong leadership. In this time of unprecedented opportunity and plentiful resources, the church is actually losing influence. The primary reason is the lack of leadership . . . Nothing is more important than leadership."

Scripture is replete with leadership models- kings, prophets, generals, administrators, strategists, visionaries, etc. So why is there so much difficulty finding exemplary leaders today? The pervasive condition of many Christian ministries imply that the demand for quality, spirit-filled, leaders constantly outweigh the supply. As a result, the on-going challenge asks the question- "What can we do about it?"

We live in a period of history where technology is at a pinnacle. Yet, with all the leadership tools that we have available- seminars, workshops, conferences, training classes, books, tapes, calendars, hand-size organizers, etc., quality leaders are still at a premium. How can that be?

Has the obvious been overlooked? Has the process of developing leaders been over-complicated? Do we need more development tools? These are all good questions; however the answer has been available to us since our Lord's earthly presence. The answer is that Jesus focuses on developing the heart and the soul of a servant-leader.

Genuine servant-leadership starts by asking- "Who am I spiritually?" When a servant-leader begins with this question, fundamental leadership development begins. In Matthew 22:34-38, the Pharisees were testing our Lord, they asked Him,

> **"Teacher, which is the greatest commandment of the Law? He responded, "You shall love your God with all of your heart, and with all of your soul, and with all of your mind."**

Similarly, in Micah 6:6-8, the nation of Israel proposed to make up for her sin by offering sacrifices, but God replied,

> **"He has told you, O man, what is good; And what does the Lord require of you, But to do justice, to love kindness, And to walk humbly with your God?"**

God cannot begin to develop a servant-leader until the heart and soul are in line with His heart, specifically when we demonstrate our love for Him.

Below, the authors of "The Leadership Baton"[2] describe the anatomy of a servant – leader:

- "Head" - To know God (a wise leader)

- "Heart" - Exhibit Christ-like character (a godly leader)

- "Hands" - Be effective in ministry and mission (a skilled leader)

Each component must work in harmony with the other. If not, overly developed parts will dominate the body and create an imbalance. For example, what would happen if you were especially gifted in studying and discerning God's word ("Head"); but, time after time you turned down opportunities to serve ("Hands") or failed to be compassionate to someone who asked for your counsel ("Heart")? That is why the goal, by God's grace, is to keep all the parts working in harmony and proportionately with each other in applying a whole-life approach in developing leaders.

The discipling approach that Jesus practiced was a whole-life application. In other words, unlike today, society tells us that we can have a "public" life and "private" life, and we can keep the two separate without any contradiction. Not so by biblical standards. Who we are on the inside must be who we are on the outside. Jesus chastised the Pharisees when he told them,

> **"Woe to you, scribes and Pharisees, hypocrites! For you are like whitewashed tombs which on the outside appear beautiful, but inside they are full of dead men's bones, and all uncleanness." Matthew 23:27.**

The opening verse of this module, Isaiah 6:8, speaks of the "Call of a Leader". The first eight verses of Isaiah 6, exemplifies how God calls leaders. God sounded a general call to anyone, but Isaiah took it personally. And, according to John Maxwell's[3] interpretation of this scripture, Isaiah responded because of three factors-

- **Opportunity** – He sees a specific place where he can make a difference. This has to do with timing (v. 1).

- **Ability** – He recognized that he had the God-given gifts to do something about the need. This has to do with competence (vv. 6-7).

- **Desire** – He wanted to step out and address the need; his hunger pushed him. This has to do with our passion (v. 8).

Isaiah's statement- "Send me!" illustrates his response to God's divine calling. He understood God's vision (vv. 1-4); he understood the vision for himself (vv. 5-7); and, he understood the vision for ministry (v. 8). The application for us through his experience is as follows:

- God revealed himself to Isaiah and he was changed forever (vv. 1-2)

- Isaiah's encounter with God helped him to realize God's holiness. God became tangible for him (vv. 3-4)

- Like Adam and Eve after the fall, he recognized his own sinfulness (v. 5)

- He acknowledged and accepted the need for a spiritual cleansing for his sins, which enabled him to serve (vv. 6-7)

- Isaiah responded to God's calling, now that he was broken and his heart was in line with God (v. 8)

As in times past, God is calling for leaders today. However, it is not until we take the time to evaluate our own lives that we can genuinely know His plan for us. Scripturally, the call to leadership has not changed. What has changed is our indifference to that calling and our unwillingness to respond according to His will. We must realize that until we approach His calling on His terms and not through our own methods, we will not be able to lead successfully. Our heart and soul must be totally submitted to Him in order serve the people He is calling us to lead.

THE MEANING OF LEADERSHIP

Leadership Defined

You can find a multitude of definitions for leadership.

- The process of influencing people to work toward the achievement of organizational objectives.

- Enabling a group to engage together in the process of developing, sharing and moving into vision, and then living it out.

- The ability to lead. The only definition of a leader is someone who has followers.

Leadership is a function of knowing yourself, having a vision that is well communicated, building trust among colleagues, and taking effective action to realize your own leadership potential. However, according to John Maxwell, "Leadership is influence- nothing more, nothing less."[4].

It appears that defining what leadership can be very illusive. We can more readily describe what leaders do, but trying to agree on what leadership is, that is another matter. If we look at leadership traits and the effectiveness of those traits, we can gain a better understanding of leadership.

Before delving into essential leadership traits that leaders possess, the common thread of all leaders must be discussed. That common thread among leaders is simply the ability to make things happen, in other words getting results. This vein runs through good as well as bad leaders. The challenge for any leader when it comes to getting results is that "outstanding results cannot be forced out of people"[5], according to Ted W. Engstrom, former president of World Vision International. Although poor leaders get results, the unknown factor that always begs the question- "What could have been accomplished under true inspirational and collaborative leadership?

Clearly, the Pharaohs of Egypt built testimonies of their legacies through all their architecture, cultural influences, artistry and riches. However, the leadership that Moses demonstrated facilitated the building of living testimonies from the children of Israel, for God, through his influence. The lesson here is that the difference between a spiritual and a worldly leader is the ability to stimulate and inspire those who follow toward a worthy and godly common goal.

Richard Wolfe writes in his book, "Man at the Top", that "when God creates a leader he is given a desire for action.[6]". It is in this way that God works in people. God's word confirms this in Philippians 2:13,

...for it is God who is at work in you, both to will and to work for His good pleasure.

The word "for" indicates that we do not work alone and also that we experience His working in us as we work for Him.

Wolfe continues his insight by stating that "prayer is not a substitute for action which flows from decision."[6]. The fact that Christ motivates leaders for action does not mean that they are passive puppets. Paul the apostle admitted that God worked in him:

But by the grace of God I am what I am, and His grace toward me did not prove vain; but I labored even more than all of them; yet not I, but the grace of God with me. I Corinthians 15:10

Paul never discounted his active participation in getting results through his ministry. However, he acknowledged that God was the force that drove him. This is why he was able to state so boldly in II Timothy 4:7- "I have fought the good fight, I have finished the course, I have kept the faith." In other words, he recognized the need and the presence of grace in his life, but he did undervalue the attributes that made him a successful leader.

Overall, the following statements are true of effective and especially spiritual leaders:

- A leader guides the activities of those with whom he or she interacts with to a positive conclusion.

- A leader is capable of performing tasks which guide people to achieving objectives.

- A leader possesses vision and faith.

- A leader demonstrates a genuine concern and a comprehensive understanding of the world around them.

- A leader will demonstrate a strong drive to take the initiative.

Natural vs. Spiritual Leadership

Before contrasting between natural and spiritual leadership gifts, we must acknowledge that both stem from the same foundation- ". . . for apart from me, you can do nothing."

John 15:5. This foundational statement speaks to the fact that God created us uniquely, thereby removing any opportunity to falsely claim that we are "self-made" and attempt to heap any glory upon ourselves.

Natural leadership refers to those characteristics which can be found inherent in individuals, such as attitude, knowledge, intuition, a sense of timing, charisma, drive, etc. Characteristics like these are typically apparent from birth. Think back to your childhood for a moment. What was your attitude towards winning and losing? Did you organize and lead the teams you played on, or did you wait to be picked? How influential were you over others?

The concern that arises from references to "natural" leadership is that it opens the door for secular thinking. Generally, secular principles and ideas have their place in developing a leader, however, if a developing leader relies on taking his or her cues from the secular marketplace over spiritual fundamentals, this can cause an identity crisis. Spiritual leaders need to be able to distinguish between God's authoritative word and worldly philosophies. Unfortunately, we see evidence that some pastors today are embracing these philosophies to the point that these philosophies become second nature, or the norm, to the detriment of their followers.

Dan Dumas, Pastor of Assimilation and Conferences at Grace Community Church emphatically states, "The church today does not need strong natural leaders. It needs strong spiritual leaders. Too many pastors are building resumes rather than people and churches."[7]

The key to a healthy understanding of our natural abilities is that with them comes an expectation of responsibility. Our Lord underscored this expectation when He stated in Luke 12:48,

. . . From everyone who has been given much, much will be required; and to whom they entrusted much, of him they will ask all the more.

The curious thing about "spiritual leadership" is that you do not find the word <u>leadership</u> anywhere in scripture. What we do find are examples of leadership and most often, those examples are associated with serving. Only once did Jesus say. "Follow my example" about something. As we read in John 13:12-17, he points out that Jesus has set an example for us. The point is that the scriptures emphasize action by serving rather than talking directly about leadership.

Servant-leadership defines spiritual leadership. It is imperative that when we are looking for leaders, we look beyond natural abilities. It's the heart of the servant that is the true test of a leader. The following passages provide examples of what God looks for in those who want to lead:

- **Matthew 20:25-28 –**

  But Jesus called them to Himself and said, "You know that the rulers of the Gentiles lord it over them, and their great men exercise authority over them. It is not this way among you, but whoever wishes to become great among you shall be your slave; just as the Son of Man did not come to be served, but to serve, and to give His life a ransom for many.

- **Mark 9:35 –**

  Sitting down, He called the twelve and said to them, "If anyone wants to be first, he shall be last of all and servant of all.

The term "spiritual leadership" implies that the Holy Spirit leads someone. This empowering of the Spirit is supernatural by nature and supersedes any natural abilities we may be relying on. The flesh wants us to draw attention to ourselves, but when we acknowledge the power of the Holy Spirit in true humility, that is when we operate at levels far exceeding our own natural capabilities.

By offering ourselves as a conduit for the Holy Spirit to work, we effectively invite the Holy Spirit to achieve what we could never do. For example, in the fourth chapter of the book of Zechariah, God's angel told Zechariah how the Temple would be finished, "Not by might, nor by power, but by my Spirit, says the Lord of host." If this fundamental truth existed then, then we too can depend on God's truth today.

God's benchmark is unselfish servanthood. Servant-leaders give up personal rights as they aspire to lead. In fact, contrary to secular business models, a spirit-filled leader's career path descends not ascends as the leadership role grows. Simply put, in God's leadership model, the way up is the way down. Servant-leadership is not a title or a position; it is a lifestyle and a calling.

J. Oswald Sanders provides us with contrasting examples of natural and spiritual leadership[8]-

Natural	Spiritual
Self-confident	Confident in God
Knows men	Also knows God
Makes own decisions	Seeks God's will
Ambitious	Humble
Creates methods	Follows God's example
Enjoys command	Delights in obedience to God
Seeks personal reward	Loves God and other
Independent	Depends on God

Because everything comes from God, Servant-Leadership synthesizes natural abilities and releases spiritual gifting to accomplish God's calling. The peripheral benefit of Servant-Leadership is that as we respond to God's calling, we serve and edify the church body. Rather than striving to be a leader, we should strive to be servants. In addition, by being servants, God considers us leaders. Luke records Paul admonition to the elders of Ephesus in Acts 20:35 that serving others is a tremendous privilege-

> **In everything I showed you that by working hard in this manner you must help the weak and remember the words of the Lord Jesus, that He himself said, 'It is more blessed to give than to receive.'**

Some additional words of encouragement:

> **"I think no servant of God is tired of serving his Master. We may be tired in the service, though not tired of it." C.H. Spurgeon**

"Most of us would have no objection to being masters. But servanthood holds little attraction." J. Oswald Sanders

Manager vs. Leader- Two Different Roles

Are you a manager or a leader? Although you may hear these two terms thrown out interchangeably, they are in fact two very different roles requiring different personalities and views.

A person can be a leader without being a manager. For example, Babe Ruth did not have managerial responsibility for planning and controlling the New York Yankees. But he frequently was called the team leader because he inspired the other team members to give superior performances.

On the other hand, a person who is a manager may not be a leader. A person is a manager by virtue of holding a formal position. Position authority by nature is the authority that "comes with the territory". It implies that whoever occupies the position acquires the authority that was given the position. Another view of authority is that unless a person's authority is not accepted by those they lead, authority is not actually present. If this is the case, then a manager cannot rely solely on position for authority.

The Babe Ruth example demonstrates that a member of a group can be an informally designated leader even though a formally appointed manager is also present. Therefore, it is through leadership skills that a manger can become a more effective.

Below we are going to take a look at the different personality styles of managers versus leaders, the attitudes each have toward goals, their basic conceptions of what work entails, and their relationships with others.

Personality styles:

Managers

- Emphasize rationality and control.

- Problem-solvers (focusing on goals, resources, organization structures, or people)

- Often ask the questions, "What problems have to be solved. "What are the best ways to achieve results so that people will continue to contribute to this organization?"

- Persistent, tough-minded, hard-working, intelligent, analytical, tolerant and have goodwill toward others.

Leaders

- Perceived as brilliant, but sometimes lonely.

- Achieve control of themselves before they try to control others.

- Can visualize a purpose and generate value in work.

- Imaginative, passionate, non-conforming risk-takers.

Attitudes toward goals:

Managers

- Adopt impersonal, almost passive, attitudes toward goals.

- Decide upon goals based on necessity instead of desire and are therefore deeply tied to their organization's culture.

- Tend to be reactive since they focus on current information.

Leaders

- Tend to be active since they envision and promote their ideas instead of reacting to current situations.

- Shape ideas instead of responding to them.

- Have a personal orientation toward goals.

- Provide a vision that alters the way people think about what is desirable, possible, and necessary.

Conceptions of work:

Managers

- View work as an enabling process.

- Establish strategies and make decisions by combining people and ideas; continually coordinate and balance opposing views.

- Are good at reaching compromises and mediating conflicts between opposing values and perspectives.

- Act to limit choice.

- Tolerate practical, mundane work because of strong survival instinct which makes them risk-averse.

Leaders

- Develop new approaches to long-standing problems and open issues to new options.

- First, use their vision to excite people and only then develop choices which give those images substance.

- Focus people on shared ideals and raise their expectations.

- Work from high-risk positions because of strong dislike of mundane work.

Relations with others:

Managers

- Prefer working with others.

- Report that solitary activity makes them anxious.

- Are collaborative; maintain a low level of emotional involvement in relationships.

- Attempt to reconcile differences, seek compromises, and establish a balance of power; relate to people according to the role they play in a sequence of events or in a decision-making process.

- Focus on how things get done; maintain controlled, rational, and equitable structures; may be viewed by others as inscrutable, detached, and manipulative.

Leaders

- Maintain inner perceptiveness that they can use in their relationships with others.

- Relate to people in intuitive, empathetic way.

- Focus on what events and decisions mean to participants.

- Attract strong feelings of identity and differences or of love and hate.

- Create systems where human relations may be turbulent, intense, and at times even disorganized.

INDIVIDUAL FACTORS OF LEADERSHIP

Traits

Stated in "Stogdill's Handbook of Leadership", "as early as the 1900's, secular management studies began to examine common leadership traits. Many of the studies were based on the premise that leaders are born, not made. Researchers wanted to identify an array of characteristics or traits that were distinctive of leaders, not followers.

Researchers studied both physical and psychological qualities, such as aggressiveness, self-reliance, appearance, dominance, etc. The purpose for identifying a group of traits was to utilize these qualities as a tool for promoting potential leaders or managers. Only those candidates possessing these qualities would be considered for leadership positions.

In 70 years over 300 trait studies were conducted. However, no universal list of traits was compiled that all successful leaders possessed. In all cases there were exceptions."[9] These exceptions varied among studies. For example, one study found that effective leaders were tall. However, Napoleon was short. Some studies showed that some leaders exhibited several of the same common traits, but many were unsuccessful in business. Peter Drucker says there is no such thing as "leadership qualities or a leadership personality."[10]. His point was that if all leaders were born and not developed, then there would be no need for courses in management.

The most widely publicized and thorough study was conducted by Edwin Ghiselli. His studies were published in 1971, which studied over 300 managers and 90 different companies in the United States. He identified six traits as being significant traits of effective leadership[11].

1. Supervisor ability – Getting the job done through others

2. A need for occupational achievement – The motivation to work hard to succeed

3. Intelligence – The ability to use good judgment, reasoning and thinking capacity

4. Decisiveness – The ability to solve problems and make decisions competently

5. Self-assurance – Behaving in a manner that show other that you have self-confidence

6. Initiative – Self-starting. Getting the job done with a minimum of supervision from one's boss

Now what does God say about the qualities of a spiritual leader? Let's take a look at two portions of scripture, please note that these particular passages are not exclusive- I Timothy 3:2-13 and Titus 1:5-9.

I Timothy 3:2-13:

1. Blameless (v. 2) – Above reproach. Integrity above all other traits is key

2. Husband of one wife (v. 2) – In the case of a Pastor or Elder. The universal application is "Am I lifting up my spouse above myself, like Jesus loved the church?"

3. Temperate and of good behavior (v. 2) – Being even-tempered and not subject to rage or irrational behavior

4. Hospitality (v. 2) – Demonstrate a genuine warm and loving attitude for those you lead

5. Able to teach (v. 2) – Take the time to teach and disciple others to "lead and feed"

6. Not given to wine (v. 3) – Sober and under control of your senses. Being an example to those around you

7. Not violent or contentious (v. 3) – Avoid quarrels and always work to be a peacemaker

8. Not greedy (v. 3) – Avoid the lust of the eyes, the flesh or worldly possessions

9. A competent overseer of one's household (vv. 4-5) – A godly manager of one's household is a prerequisite before managing God's house

10. Not new to the faith (v. 6) – Rapid advancement can cause pride to stumble a new leader. Maturity in the faith minimizes problems.

Titus 1:5-9: Traits that deal with personal character, rather than gifts or skills-

1. Personal life: Blameless, not self-willed or quick tempered, not violent

2. Family life: Faithfull to your spouse and children

3. Social life: Hospitable, not given to wine

4. Financial life: A steward of God, not greedy for money

5. Professional life: Not insubordinate, just, faithful to the Word, able to exhort and convict those who contradict God's Word

What is important to note, Paul wrote in I Timothy 3:10- "These men must also first be tested." This must be a pre-requisite before being appointed to a leadership position. It is critical that time be spent to develop and observe those who aspire to greater responsibilities. If this initial principal is overlooked, then the door is opened to potential problems.

Frank Damazio senior pastor of City Bible Church in Portland, Oregon, illustrates Paul's logic concerning leadership:

Leader's Salvation	Leader's Call	Leader's Preparation	Leader's Position
Leadership is planted as a seed	Leadership begins to grow	Leadership is tested as a plant	Leadership matures and bears fruit

There is a balance between a born leader and a developed leader. The contrast is similar to the question, "Is experience more important than education or vise-a versa?" As with most things, there is a balance. There are traits within leaders which the Lord has created within them, however, we never stop learning. Leadership experience enhances those natural traits and spiritual development comes through God's Word.

Beliefs and Values

Values represent the way we ought to behave, and beliefs represent if-then statements. If I do X, then Y will happen. Values and beliefs provide the operating principles that guide decision-making and behaviors. We can observe behavior, but not values and beliefs. We can only infer from peoples' behavior what they value and believe. Secular leadership's values and beliefs can come from anywhere and are at best situational. However, in God's economy, a spiritual leader's values and beliefs are derived from is Word and it never changes.

King David, in Psalm 15:1-5 describes for us what value-driven leadership looks like. The doorkeepers to the values written in this Psalm are integrity and righteousness. These values give us access to God in his tabernacle.

- A leader walks uprightly (v.2) – Integrity is a fundamental value

- A leader works righteousness (v.2) – Demonstrated deeds speak for themselves

- A leader speaks the truth (v.2) – Lies are not an option. Your yes is your yes and your no is your no.

- A leader does not slander with his tongue, nor does he do evil to his neighbor (v.3) – Love your neighbor as yourself (Leviticus 19:18)

- A leader despises wrongdoing (v.4) – Speak up against what is wrong

- A leader keeps his word (v.4) – Even when it costs you

- A leader is not greedy or takes bribes (v.5) – Gain at the expense of others is not acceptable

These values are not natural to man. They are bestowed upon those who seek His face. As a result, as stated in verse 1, a spiritual leader whose values are driven by God's Word can expect to abide and dwell with God forever.

Styles of Leadership

According to a report by the American Management Association, the majority of the managers who participated in the survey agreed that the most important single skill of a leader is the ability to have a good relationship with people. They also rated this skill above intelligence, decisiveness, knowledge, or job skills.

Leadership style is defined as the way a leader carries out his or her functions and how those they lead look them upon. How people perceive a leader is more of a reality than any skill sets or gifting a leader possesses. If a leader is perceived as an ineffective leader, no degree, special talents or level of authority will gain the confidence or loyalty of those they oversee.

Adaptability is a key component to effective leadership. The more flexible a leader's style as it adapts to a particular situation or the needs of people, the more efficiently goals will be met and tasks completed. Leadership style is just as important as a leader's purpose or philosophy. Successful leaders adapt their leadership behavior to meet the needs of people and situations.

The descriptors as described by Robert N. Lussier, for various styles of leadership vary, however they all can be summarized into the following categories[12]:

1. Active leadership: Personally involved in the day-to-day activities of the organization and employees.

2. Democratic leadership: Works for consensus of opinions and fosters trust harmony and job-satisfaction.

3. Directive leadership: Does not usually solicit employee input. Tends to act unilaterally.

4. Paternalistic leadership: Although these leaders are concerned with their employees' wellbeing, the needs of the organization come first.

5. Participatory leadership: The leader acts as a coach. The focus is on empowering employees to seek knowledge and solutions on their own.

6. Task-oriented leadership: These leaders focus on planning and implementation of tasks. Strict deadlines for progress are paramount.

7. Servant leadership: This management looks to find the most talented people to run the organization and then empowers them to do their jobs. This manager sees his position as a servant to his/her employees and customers.

Now the question is, "Which style is best?" Because leaders and subordinates are different, so are the styles in a given situation or group setting. Some situations require one style of leadership, while others require another style. The appropriate style depends on the task, the people being managed, the organizational environment and the need at the moment.

The phase of life of an organization also plays a part in which leadership style best fits tasks and needs. For example, during a phase of rapid growth and expansion, autocratic leadership may work well. This can be seen when a new church plant is established by a pastor who is a visionary, charismatic, who knows intuitively what is to be done and how to do it. Since the vision is his, he is in the best position to crystallize all the steps necessary to develop the vision.

On the other hand, during a slow growth or maturity phase of an organization, participative leadership may be the most effective. Including more individuals in the decision-making process at this stage enables the visionary to delegate lower priority activities and concentrate on future endeavors. The needs of the moment dictate the management style that best meets those needs.

Flexibility is the key. There are advantages and disadvantages to each style. Each style must be understood and evaluated against real life situations. A mature leader has an advantage because he or she is not bound by any one style. An experienced and mature leader will not feel threatened or intimidated as various styles are utilized.

Ted Engstrom points out that what is more vital than style is recognizing levels of priority for Christian leadership. He emphasizes that the order is crucial as well[13]-

1. Our commitment to the person of God in Christ - This is because of our personal relationship with Jesus, the Son of God

2. Our commitment to the body of Christ – The measure of a Christian is our love for one another because the body of Christ has many parts.

3. Our commitment to the work of Christ or the task that the Lord has given us – Although we are called to sacrifice possessions and families to follow Christ, the work of Christ will flow forth from the relationships that exist. God considers our relationship with Him and others more important than our accomplishments. God will get His work done.

TYPES OF BEHAVIORAL LEADERSHIP

Researchers who have studied leadership behavior have identified four general individual types of leadership behaviors according to Robert N. Lussier in his book "Management: Concepts, Applications, Skills Development".[14]

Charismatic Leadership

This leadership behavior inspires loyalty, enthusiasm, and high levels of performance. Examples of charismatic leader, such as; Martin Luther King, Jr., Lee Iacocca, John F. Kennedy, Billy Graham and John Calvin.

Some of the common characteristics they possess are idealized goals or vision, a strong personal commitment to their goals or vision, an ability to communicate their goals or vision, then display a strong confidence and are able to make radical changes.

Followers, in turn, trust theses leaders so much that they believe and adopt their goals or vision, feel affection for them, develop an emotional involvement for their goal or vision and develop a strong desire to perform.

Transformational Leader

This leadership behavior is based on change, innovation, entrepreneurship and continually moves an organization into three areas:

1. Organizational revitalization: the transformational leader recognizes the need to change the organization in order to keep up with the rapid changes in their environment. They are challenged to keep either in line with or ahead of their competition.

2. Creating new vision: the transformational leader visualizes the changes occurring in an organization and motivates people to make those changes happen.

3. Institutional change: the transformational leader guides people as they make the vision a reality.

Transactional Leader

This leadership behavior is based on leadership style and exchange. This exchange is based on the principle that, "If you do the work for me and I'll reward you". This type of leader can be found most often at levels of middle or first-line manager. These levels of leadership have very limited authority and scope.

Symbolic Leadership

This leadership behavior relies on establishing and maintaining a strong organizational culture. Followers learn the culture and share values, beliefs, and assumptions about how they should behave in the organization. Symbolic leadership begins at the top level and cascades down.

RESPONSIBILITIES OF LEADERSHIP

Managing daily pressures are one of many job descriptors of leadership. Typically, these pressures are a result of a leader's concern for the organization, subordinates, or the goals which have been established. A leader's ability to understand and accept the responsibilities attached to their role enables a leader to decide early on if this calling is for them.

The following are some responsibilities, which a leader must consider before pursuing this calling.

1. **Set and achieve goals.**

   A leader at every level is given the responsibility to achieve specific, measurable goals and objectives. The inability to get the required results, and to achieve the goals in a timely fashion, are the primary reasons for failure and frustration in any size organization.

2. **Solve problems and make decisions.**

   Whatever leadership role you play within your organization or ministry, the title that appears on your business card can be crossed out and replaced with the words, "Problem-Solver." This is your real job. In solving problems, think and talk exclusively in terms of solutions. Focus all your attention on the specific actions you can take to solve the problem. Forget about the past and who is to blame. Focus on the future and what actions you can take now.

3. **Set priorities and work on key tasks.**

   One of your key responsibilities is to work on your most vital task at all times and to assure that everyone who reports to you is also working on their key tasks. Always ask yourself, "What are my highest value activities?" If you could only do one thing all day long, what one task would that be?

4. **Possess a genuine concern for others**

   Place the needs of others over your own. Lead them through your confidence in the Lord to give them hope in their most stressful trials. Show sympathy and compassion for those who need your strength which He as given you.

5. **Provide a vision for others**

   In order for the sheep to follow, the Shepherd must know where he is going. Paul the apostle said, "Follow my example as I follow the example of Christ" (I Corinthians 11:1). Even in the most challenging trials, keeping sight of the vision which the Lord has given you will minimize doubt and discouragement. Keep your line of sight, and stay the course according to His will.

6. **Be a role model for others.**

   This is perhaps the most important responsibility of leadership. Leaders must conduct themselves as though everyone is watching them even when no one is watching. Godly leaders set higher standards for themselves than others would set for them. Nothing contributes more to unity of command than for subordinates to work under someone they greatly respect and admire. Your commitment to being a servant-leader and demonstrating godly values is the most important quality of leadership.

CHALLENGES AND PITFALLS OF LEADERSHIP

Just as sheep beget sheep, so does poor leadership beget poor leadership. The example that leaders exhibit is surely followed by those who admire and respect them. This is especially true of young, inexperienced, and sometimes very trusting subordinates. Of the many traits that God looks for in a leader one of the most important is finding someone who will stand in the gap (Ezekiel 22:24-31). Specifically, God is looking for someone who will bridge the gap between His people and Himself. From church ministries to secular companies to political parties, all are looking for leaders to fill the empty slots with integrity.

In order for the "law of reproduction" to be godly and effective, a leader must serve as a point man for his followers and identify the landmines that lie ahead. Afterwards, a servant-leader can guide them and teach them how to look for those same pitfalls. The following is a sampling of pitfalls and mistakes that a leader should recognize. The first four are observations from J. Oswald Sanders[15] and the following five are observations from Hans Finzel[14].

- Pride – If gone unchecked, the attitude will disqualify a leader from further advancement in the kingdom. The Lord detests all the proud of heart (Proverbs 16:5)

- Jealousy – A near relative of pride describes the person who is suspicious of rivals. Moses faced the same issue with Joshua in Numbers 11:27-29. Envy and jealousy have no place in the kingdom of God. As followers of Christ, we all are working towards the same goal- perpetuating God's Word.

- Infallibility – Spirituality does not guarantee infallible judgment. The Spirit-filled leader is less likely to make mistakes in judgment than his secular counterpart is, but perfection eludes us all.

- Indispensability – Many leaders fall into this temptation. It appears that Christian leaders are especially prone to this pitfall. They cling on to authority or position long after it should have been passed on to younger leaders. The real negative consequence is that younger leaders who have the energy, are held back and stagnated. As a result, they tend to move on to other ministries who offer them an opportunity, when they could have been retained.

- Top-down Attitude – This is characterized by the person who believes that everyone should serve him, as opposed to him serving others. Effective leaders see themselves at the bottom of an inverted pyramid.

- Dictatorship in Decision-making – Dictators denies the values of others. As a leader's responsibilities increase, the more the leader should recognize the genuine value of those he or she leads. A leader who facilitates those he or she leads says, "My job is to help those I lead release as much of their potential as possible.

- Refusing to Adequately Delegate – "Over managing is one of the greatest sins of leadership." Nothing frustrates people more than sloppy delegation with too many strings attached. Delegation should match each person's abilities.

- Success without Successors – Begin planning your departure from the beginning. Pride tightens the grip on leadership; humility relaxes and lets go. Mentoring is an essential function for successful leadership.

COST OF LEADERSHIP

The story is told about a man who asked a stranger what time it was. The stranger put down his two heavy suitcases, looked at his watch and said, "It is now 5:09 p.m., the temperature outside is 73 degrees, and it is going to rain tonight." Surprised, the man said, "Wow, your watch tells you all that? I'd like to buy it. Here's $200." The stranger said "no." But the man insisted and offered $1,000. Finally, the stranger agreed. Happy with his new watch, the man wore it on his wrist and turned to leave, whereupon the stranger handed him the two heavy suitcases and said, "Hey, don't forget the batteries!"

The problem of many followers or would-be-followers of Christ is that they become too focused on the wristwatch, and they forget the heavy batteries that come along with it. Too focused on the perks, they forget the work. Too engrossed in the privileges, they forget the cost. They forget there is a price for true discipleship and leadership. In today's Gospel (Luke. 9:61-62) Jesus reminds His disciples that anyone who follows Him must have the 3 S's: Sincerity, sacrifice and service.

Leadership is both a privilege and a high calling. However, it also comes with a cost. Can you pay the price? It is not unusual for people to desire to lead, however sometimes the sacrifices and hardships are not completely taken into consideration. Those seeking status, position and recognition, especially in ministry, wash out quickly and sometimes stumble others along the way.

If anyone is thinking about going into the front lines of battle as a leader in ministry, first consider Jesus' parable about a king preparing for war:

Will he not first sit down and consider whether he is able with ten thousand men to oppose the one coming against him with twenty thousand? If he is not able, he will send a delegation while the other is still a long way off and will ask for terms of peace (Luke 14:31-32).

Ask yourself the same question that the Lord posed to James and John in Mark 10:35-38, "… are you able to drink the cup that I drink?"

Many see the rewards of leadership, but do not realize or see the sacrifices in following Him. The greater the calling, the greater the toll, especially if your ministry is effective. The cost is not always paid in lump sums. More often it is done in payments, day-after-day.

Her are three general areas of cost that every potential leader should weigh-

- Physical Cost – theses costs come in the forms a sacrifice of your time, your finances or lack of finances, privacy, health and any tangible asset you hold dear

- Emotional Cost – Conflict is a major cost contributor. Although not all conflict is bad, when it is bad it can take its toll well beyond our comfort level. Emotion deals with feelings. Therefore, it is not unusual for a leader to encounter extraordinary episodes of hurt, frustration and angry feelings. Add to that; feelings of loneliness, rejection, and sometimes failure.

- Spiritual Cost - Satan is not all-powerful, but he is no dummy either. He knows that if he can bump off the shepherd, the sheep will be nearly helpless. Leaders in battle are more likely to be hit by a bullet because they are out in front where the ammunition is flying. Three common areas of attack come from sexual temptation, unresolved conflict among leaders and pride. Fortunately, we have the weapons to fight back. Prayer, reading His Word, and collaborating with someone that will hold us accountable are our defense.

Let's look as some specific cost factors of leadership-

1. **Self-sacrifice**

   Jesus made it very clear that He and His followers were not out for a joy ride. Anyone who wants to follow Him must be ready to take up the cross and embrace deprivations, humiliations and even goodbyes for the sake of the Kingdom. Disciples or leaders who do not know self-denial do more harm than good to the people whom they claim to serve. If there is no suffering in the life of a disciple or a leader, then we must question his/her authenticity and credibility.

   Self-sacrifice is paid daily. We are called to pick up our crosses and follow Him. In doing so, we deny ourselves what we think is important and look to see from an eternal kingdom perspective.

   In Mark 1:19-20, we see a model sacrifice illustrated of the apostles. Mark tells us that James and John were called out by Jesus and they left their father. Their response to God's calling was immediate and without any reservations. These men set aside what, for most of us, is most precious, our family. Yet, they responded without question, regret or fear. It is not the Lord's intention to cause dysfunctional families. However, He made it very clear to all His creation when he stated in the His first commandment- "You shall have no other Gods before Me" (Exodus 20:3). This includes our families.

   In order to begin to understand the sacrifice and dedication required of a leader, three needs should be fulfilled as a part of servant-ministry-

   1. First, a leader <u>needs</u> to believe that Jesus is real in his or her life. A leader willingly loves and serves Him first and above all else, without any reservations. When a leader has a genuine relationship with the Lord, then others around them can begin to see them in a different light. It's when a leader is inconsistent in their walk that loved ones become confused and frustrated with a leader. A dedicated life of a leader defines them for others.

2. Second, a leader <u>needs</u> to impart to his/her family and friends that Jesus should be real in their lives. By doing so they will come to know what is expected of them and have a clearer understanding of the leader's priority in life

3. Third, a leader <u>needs</u> to convey to a skeptical world that God can be real in their lives through a faith in Jesus Christ. When the world sees a leader's commitment to Christ, then the world can start to question the significance of this world and how it relates to an eternal creator. At the risk of stirring up controversy, a leader can use any witnessing opportunity to stimulate discussion about a loving Savior.

2. Criticism

A great price is paid when criticism is cast upon us. The inability to cope with criticism is a sign of emotional immaturity. When this shortfall is ignored, it can affect not only the leader but also the people around them and the progress of a common goal.

Conversely, constructive feedback is the counterpart to disparaging criticism. Healthy feedback from others helps us to see more clearly. At times leaders need comments from others, especially those they trust. As leaders analyze the comments, they can appropriately digest and disseminate the information and revise those areas, which need improving.

Beware of flattery, it can be deceiving. One definition of flattery is "something someone says to our face that they wouldn't say behind our backs!" Backslappers make us feel good about ourselves for the moment, but in the long run, their comments are not of much value. More importantly, we must never believe the flattering tongue. Proverbs 26:28 reminds us- "A lying tongue hates those it crushes, and a flattering mouth works ruin."

3. Fatigue

It's been said that tired men and women run the world. There may be some truth to that, because committed leaders have to rise early, study longer, go further and stay later as a way to distinguish themselves from those who are not passionate about their calling.

Fatigue is inevitable in our lives. It is part of the weakened condition of our natural, sinful state. However, "burn-out" is not a result of a spiritual calling. When we are working under our own strength rather than His, we are on a collision course with burnout.

A balanced walk reflects that we are doing our part, and we are letting God do His part. A balanced leader will seek rest and recreation in his or her calling. The Lord's most significant example for us is that He "rested" on the seventh day. Not that He was fatigued, but He ceased to work; no weariness was implied. So for us, we need to cease from work in order to refresh ourselves, bond with our loved ones and provide ourselves with temporary distractions to prepare us for the work ahead.

4. Loneliness

A true and confident leader promotes others in their interests, mission, goals, etc. As a result, often the leader is left alone to pursue his/her own calling. This is due to the fact that a leader and visionary cannot be caught up in the group. A leader most often is a pioneer and that means stepping out into uncharted territories alone. However, it is through those periods of solitude that God can reveal Himself and His plans for us without distractions.

Standing alone at times takes great courage. Elijah demonstrated that courage when he announced God's judgment to a sinful nation, confronted a wicked king and stood before a host of false prophets and challenged their godliness (I Kings 17:1-18:40). In his stand, Elijah demonstrated visual proof of the impotency of Israel's idolatress worship to Baal. For leaders today, the lesson is that there will be times when standing alone is the only option, especially when speaking a difficult truth.

There must be a balance in order for a leader to be effective. The leader must be able to identify with those he/she leads and allow for times of isolation. If the scales are tipped too much to one side or the other, then those inequities begin to hinder valuable relationships, which are much needed.

Emotional stability is key. A leader must be able to develop healthy friendships and be at the ready when those relationships take a different tack. It is through a well-developed emotional maturity that maintains the leader when all have abandoned him or her in light of a decision, a vision, an idea or a true conviction that the Lord has placed on their heart. This means that standing firm can often be lonely.

5. Rejection

Any Christian, especially a Christian leader, must be ready to pay the price of rejection. There is always the potential that a leader will be ostracized for their conviction or calling. However, we are comforted by our Lord's life of rejection, "He came to His own, and those who were His own did not receive Him." (John 1:11)

Personal courage is a major asset in the life of a leader. And that courage comes from a healthy and genuine relation with Christ our Savior. For it is through Him that we can do all things and apart from Him we can do nothing. Fear can be paralyzing, but it doesn't have to control or defeat us. We, through the power of the Holy Spirit, can overcome obstacles that we cannot picture our in our mind's eye. When we lay hold of God's promises, then we move forward in victory.

To help overcome rejection, a leader must learn to lean on Christ. We have the ability to draw on our Lord when rejection, loneliness and depression cross our path and turn those adversities into opportunities for the kingdom. As long as leaders remember that, ". . . greater is He that is in you than he who is in the world." (I John 4:4)

Finally, and most importantly, there is power in weakness. We must recognize our poverty before God. It may sound like a contradiction for a *lack* of something to be a resource. However, such is the nature of our relationship with God. When we rely on ourselves, we do not allow God to give us his strength.

Even though we leaders are quick to say we are saved by grace (God's strength), not works (our strength), we act like all that changes when we are living out the Christian life. In actuality, we are just as helpless to lead a holy life without God as we were to enter into that new life in the first place. We must trust in the Lord in all circumstances.

<u>What is the cost of leadership these days?</u> It's difficult to say because it is different for everyone. What can be said is that true leadership and true discipleship entail sacrifice and <u>self-denial for the Kingdom of God. It involves a lot of letting go of what you could have</u> kept, a lot of letting be of that which you could have controlled, and a lot of letting God instead of letting me.

References:

1. John Maxwell, "The Maxwell Leadership Bible", Thomas Nelson Bibles, 2002, VII - Introduction

2. Rowland Forman, Jeff Jones, Bruce Miller, "The Leadership Baton", Zondervan, 2004, Grand Rapids, IL, p. 62

3. Maxwell, op. cit., p. 816.

4. Maxwell, op. cit., page viii

5. Ted Engstrom, "The Making of a Christian Leader", Zondervan Publishing, 1976, Grand Rapids, Michigan, p. 20.

6. Richard Wolfe, "Man on the Top", Tyndale House Publishers, Wheaton, Ill., 1969, p. 43.

7. Dan Dumas, 2003 Shepherds' Conference, Handout-Study Notes for "Developing a Servant-Driven Church", Grace Community Church, 2003, www.biblebb.com/files/MAC/SC03-1052CDNotes.htm

8. J. Oswald Sanders, "Spiritual Leadership", Moody Press, 1994, Chicago, ILL, p. 29

9. Bernard Bass, "Stogdill's Handbook of Leadership", rev. ed., New York, Frees Press, 1981

10. Peter Drucker, "Leadership: More Doing Than Dash", The Wall Street Journal, January 6, 1988, p. 24

11. Edwin Ghiselli, "Exploration in Management Talent." (Santa Monica, CA: Goodyear, 1971).

12. Robert N. Lussier, "Management: Concepts, Applications, Skill Development, International Thompson Publishing, 1997, p. 396-397

13. Edward Dayton & Ted Engstrom, "Strategy for Leadership", Fleming H. Revell Company, Old Tappan New Jersey, 1979, p. 71

14. Op Cit, Robert N. Lussier, "Management: Concepts, Applications, Skill Development, International Thompson Publishing, 1997, p. 396-397

15. J. Oswald Sanders, Op Cit, p. 153-157

16. Hans Finzel, "The Top Ten Mistakes Leaders Make", Cooks Communications Ministries, Colorado Springs, CO, 2000, pp. 29, 82-96, 103, 157-177

SUMMARY

Godly leadership is the only means of leaving a legacy, which will live well beyond any leader's life span. Not all are called to lead, but all are called to serve. It is every leader's responsibility to serve as a living model of our Lord's life. Moreover, the reason we do that is to humble ourselves before God and those we lead.

We can talk about what makes a leader, such as traits, beliefs, values, skills, character, etc., but the core of leadership is service. A leader can possess a multitude of talents and gifts, but without the heart of a servant, they are meaningless.

There is no greater gift than that of love. If love is not the driving factor in all that a leader does, then there is no way that he or she can be truly effective for the kingdom. The world tells us that leaders are found at the top of the pyramid, but in God's kingdom, a leader is at the bottom of an inverted pyramid.

A servant is not greater than his Master (Matthew 10:24). Responding to the call to lead means starting at the bottom. Christ came to us in total humility. He set aside his kingship to lead us. This is what is at the core of true godly leadership. When leaders find themselves sacrificing their time, finances, egos, and needs, then their calling will truly be rewarding.

Many are called, but few are chosen (Matthew 22:1-14). This is especially true of those who say they are called to leadership, but only wish to be served. Those people will be weeded out in time and exposed for their selfish motives. Count the cost before stepping forward to lead.

PERSONAL APPLICATION

1. Explain, who is responsible for developing leaders? Back up your answer with scripture.

2. Explain the church's role in developing leaders. Back up your answer with scripture.

3. Explain what you are doing to develop or disciple someone currently (one page or less)

4. Find two scriptural examples of a leader and the sacrifice they made

5. In two to three paragraphs, explain what sacrifices you have to make in following Christ

6. In two to three paragraphs explain what sacrifices you foresee and are prepared to experience by your involvement in the Leadership First – School of Ministry

7. Read "Spiritual Leadership" by J. Oswald Sanders.

Ministry Financial Stewardship

Let a man regard us in this manner, as servants of Christ and stewards of the mysteries of God. In this case, moreover, it is required of stewards that one be found trustworthy. I Corinthians 4:1-2

This module is designed to give non-financially inclined leaders both an overall perspective of managing ministry finances and some strategic insights. The goal is to give a working manager's perspective rather than train up an accountant. That level of training is well beyond the scope of this module due to the complex nature of detailed financial management.

CHALLENGES TO GOOD STEWARDSHIP

There are a number of character traits that are important for any prudent financial steward. Being trustworthy should be at the

top of that list. Webster's defines trustworthy as, "worthy of confidence" or "dependable". Luke writes, "Therefore if you have not been faithful in the use of unrighteous mammon, who will entrust the true riches to you?" Restated, if a steward cannot be responsible in man's economy, how can that steward be entrusted with spiritual responsibilities- "true riches"?

The best ally for any steward is plain old common sense! It is very easy to get caught up in the zeal of wanting to enhance a church ministry by purchasing assets which can be perceived as "needed", or developing expensive programs which will more effectively "minister" to the body of Christ, or encumber a large mortgage for the sake of "accommodating" more believers, etc. Even with the best intentions, if sound judgment is not applied, mismanaging God's provisions can deprive or short-change genuine needs within the church body.

The challenges that any ministry encounters always have the potential to act outside of the will of God. Trusting in God's timing often causes us to contemplate moving ahead of God. When we do, the results are always less than what He would have provided and He

is robbed of the glory that should have been His. We need to remember the words of James 1:4- "And let endurance have its perfect result, so that you may be perfect and complete, lacking in nothing."

The prudent steward will establish safeguards that will enable him or her to think through financial challenges before making a decision. One safeguard is to surround yourself with wise counsel. That wise counsel can come from fellow pastors, ministry leaders, an Elder board, a Business board, your spouse or even a trusted friend. Any one of these advisors can be utilized, but the key is to listen to them and seriously consider their advice. After considering the advice, carefully spend time in prayer to seek the Lord's direction and will.

Another helpful process is to ask yourself some important questions as you begin to deliberate on any significant financial matter at hand. Ask yourself-

- "What is my true motive for considering this financial matter"
- "Does my desired outcome tie to the Mission and Vision that God gave me for this ministry?"

- "What will be impacted in pursuing this decision?"

- "Do I have to act on this now, or can I wait?"

- "How practical is my desired outcome or are other options available to provide the same results with less impact?"

By taking the time to meditate on the answers to these questions, you can begin to weigh all the information available to make the best decision. These questions are not all-inclusive. Be open to other questions as the Lord guides your decision process.

MISSION, VISION AND PLANNING

The first priority in planning the financial goals and infrastructure of any ministry is prayer and reflection in seeking God's will for the ministry. Too often, decision makers-pastors, elders, business board members- focus directly on the income and expenses, rather than the vision that God has revealed for his people.

Church ministry goals begin with God's shepherd for his people- the pastor. He/she is responsible for seeking the Lord's direction and the church's unique purpose for the Body of Christ and the community at-large. The pastor is the vision catcher and the Body of Christ is the agent who fulfills God's calling as He provides. Proverbs 29:18 tells us that where there is no vision, people will go unrestrained and that may result in fatal circumstances. The unrestrained actions of financial stewards can manifest themselves, for example, in indulgent spending, unnecessary debt, a poor perspective of tithing, financial mismanagement, and more. All of which can lead to an anemic relationship with God and the eventual removal of His presence in the life of a church.

As the pastor seeks God's direction for the vision and mission of the ministry, it is important for him to remember that God may be speaking to others within the body about ministry opportunities. Ministry leaders should be encouraged to pray about what God is speaking to them specifically about their own ministry. Ministry leaders typically are more intimately involved with the people they serve, which allows them to monitor the pulse of ministry more accurately.

Vision extends to all those who seek God's will. Just as a pastor receives God's revelation for the church, ministry leaders, volunteers, and the body at large can receive God's guidance for a specific work within the church. God can and does speak through others in a healthy church. However, the challenge for any pastor is discerning what is of God and what is of the flesh.

The tools that aid a pastor in discerning what is of God and relevant to the ministry is the Mission and Vision of the church which God has given him. Because God is not the

author of confusion, He will not create contradictions within the church. That is why the words given to Habakkuk are relevant for us today- "Then the Lord answered me and said, 'Record the vision and inscribe it on tablets, that the one who reads it may run. For the vision is yet for the appointed time; it hastens toward the goal and it will not fail. Though it tarries, wait for it; for it will certainly come, it will not delay.'"

For that reason, the priority for a pastor should be to seek God's vision and mission for the church and then document it for future guidance. Then, it is the pastor's responsibility to articulate it to the body. By communicating the vision and mission, the people can now readily use the vision and mission statement to benchmark new and creative ideas as they arise. If a new idea or vision aligns with the vision and mission of the church, then it is the responsibility of the pastor to fully pray when considering the recommendation. Through his discernment and possibly godly counsel, he can determine the next steps.

BUDGETING FUNDAMENTALS

"Budget, who needs a budget?" "Where God leads, He provides." "Budgets stifle the work of the Holy Spirit." Aren't all these valid statements? Do these statements challenge our faith in God? How do we reconcile our trust in God with conventional wisdom?

Practically speaking, budgets or spending plans are the prudent tool which enables financial stewards to reconcile needs with vision. Proverbs provide us with two jewels of wisdom-

> **"Poor is he who works with a negligent hand, but the hand of the diligent makes rich." Proverbs 10:4**

> **"He also who is slack in his work is brother to him who destroys." Proverbs 18:9**

The point is that we need to be diligent in the financial affairs of the church, which the Lord has entrusted to us. By strategically developing a spending plan, a roadmap is created to manage the needs of the church. A budget prepares a ministry for anticipated expenses and if properly crafted makes allowances for the unexpected expenses.

The key to a healthy perspective of the budgeting process is to remember that nothing should be set in stone. Be flexible and be willing to adjust the initial spending plan when

unforeseen activities occur or when the Spirit leads in a different direction. A steward's sensitivity to the leading of the Holy Spirit challenges those whose school of thought demands financial projections. Although secular business thrives on such

projections, in God's economy, such projections tend to move the focus to the vision of tomorrow and away from the needs of today.

That's not to say that if the Lord has given a pastor the vision for a school or a new building for example, it should be ignored. On the contrary, plans should be made in relation to the ministry's mission and vision statement, and relative to the current ongoing needs of the church.

Some financial stewards consider the budget process a necessary evil. Many would rather have root canal than tie up any time in the annual budget process. Some of the negative connotations associated with the budgeting process are:

- The process is too lengthy

- There is too much financial restraint and control

- Financial expertise is necessary to design an effective plan

- A budget is too difficult to manage

A budget doesn't dictate what has to be done, it should conform to your plans. A spending plan actually has a biblical foundation. In Luke 14:28, he states that if a man builds a tower, then he needs to count the cost. Actually, by counting the cost, the first consideration should be, "Do we need to build this tower?" Just because you have the provisions to build the tower, add staff members, or purchase additional sound equipment, etc., does not mean you need to. Simply stated, plan carefully first, then budget second!

The essential steps in developing a ministry budget are:

1. Pray and seek God's counsel in developing a vision and mission statement to accomplish His will through the Body of Christ

2. Set goals and objectives

3. Establish priorities

4. Estimate God's provision (income)

5. Estimate ministry needs (expenses)

6. Balance the budget. Get the projected expenses equal or lower than the expected projected provisions

In summary, a budget needs to be flexible and capable of accommodating change. Keep in mind that people control budgets, not visa-versa. The amounts that are inserted in the budget line items are at best, well thought out projections based upon past performance or

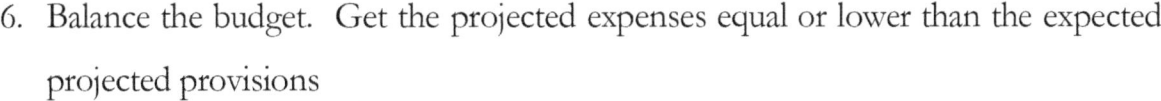

activities. The budgeting process can be an exact science, but the data that populates it is not.

Good financial stewards need to include input from those who will be directly responsible for ministry oversight. Remember, you cannot hold accountable ministry leaders who have no knowledge of unrealistic or un-communicated goals. Ministry leaders need to know they are part of the budgeting process in order to gain their buy-in and understand not only their respective budget responsibility, but also how budget provisions and expenses affect the overall budget.

BOOKKEEPING OR ACCOUNTING?

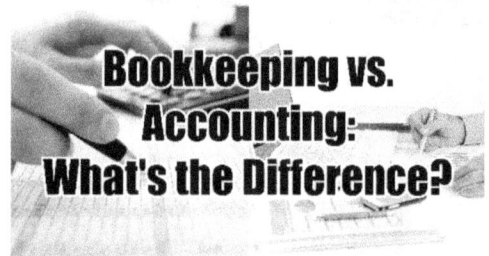

Bookkeeping, by definition, is the process of recording business transactions in a regular and systematic manner, so as to show their relation to each other, reeling the state of the business in which they occur. The books commonly used are a checkbook, journal, and ledger.

Accounting on the other hand is defined as the system of recording and summarizing business and financial transactions and analyzing, verifying, and reporting the results.

Do the definitions sound similar and maybe confusing to you? Don't worry, you are not alone. Bookkeeping is the functional aspect of tracking the financial activities of an organization. A "Bookkeeper" records the day-to-day transactions of an organization, such as money that was received or the bill that was paid. Bookkeeping concentrates on the transactional events, which are recorded on a specific time interval, such as daily, monthly, quarterly, etc.

Accounting on the other hand refers to the formal process or methodology of preparing and interpreting financial records. The emphasis is on interpretation. The "Accountant" is responsible for applying the principles of accounting in preparing financial statements or interpreting financial information so that decisions can be made. Bookkeeping deals with the "how and when" and accounting deals with the "why and what does it mean".

For the purpose of this module, we will be dealing with accounting as a function relating to interpreting financial information.

ACCOUNTNG BASICS

The Accounting Equation

Accounting is based on three fundamental elements: assets, liabilities and equity. *Assets* are anything of monetary value that a business or ministry owns. The most common assets are cash, securities, property (land, building, furniture, etc.), office equipment, etc.

Liabilities are any debts that a business or ministry owes. The most common liabilities are mortgage loans, purchases bought on credit, employee salaries that are due in the future, employee taxes due to government agencies, etc.

Equity is the financial interest of a business or ministry. Equity is defined as the difference between the assets and the liabilities of a business or ministry. The relationship of the accounting equation is illustrated in the graphic below:

BALANCE SHEET

Assets				=	Liabilities	+	Equity
Checking Acct.	Savings Acct.	Furniture	Office Equipment		Mortgage		Net Assets
$175,000 +	$225,000 +	$7,500 +	$3,600	=	$275,000	+	$136,100
	$411,100			=		$411,100	

ACCOUNTING CYCLE

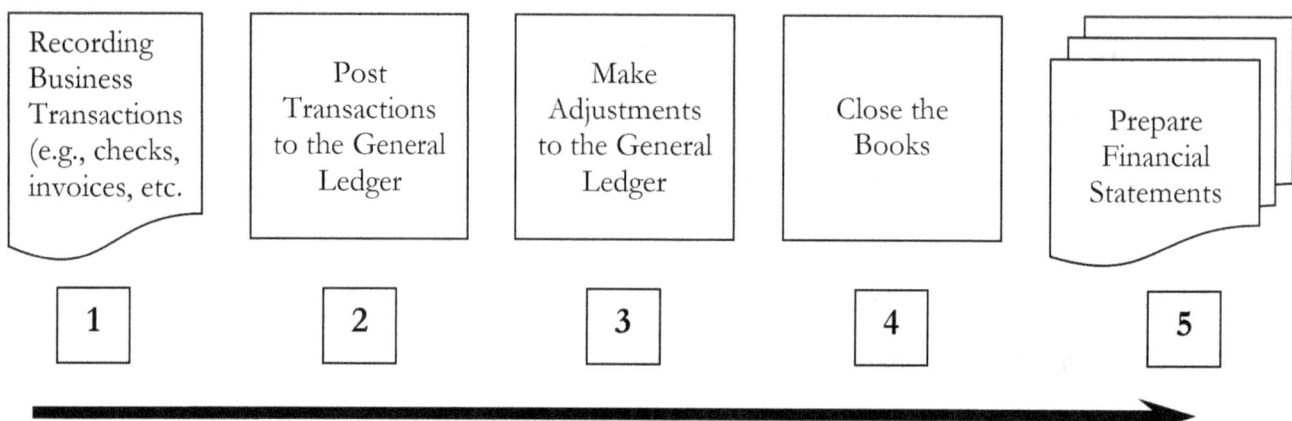

Before you can set up your accounting records, you must dive into your day-to-day transactions, get your books ready for end-of-month or end-of-year reporting, you must gain an understanding of basic accounting concepts.

As previously stated, accounting is the method by which financial information is gathered, processed, and summarized into financial statements and reports. The process is conducted over specific periods of time, such monthly, quarterly or annually. As illustrated above, the basic accounting cycle includes.

1. **Recording business transactions.**

   Recording original source documents such as checks, billing invoices, and payroll timesheets are all examples of the initial step of the accounting cycle. Businesses keep a daily record of chronological transactions in a general journal, cash-receipt journal or a cash-disbursement journal.

2. **Posting debits and credits to a general ledger.**

   The general ledger is a summary of all balance sheet, income, and expense accounts used to keep a business's accounting records. An up-to-date general ledger shows current information about accounts payable, accounts receivable, owners' equity and other accounts. At the end of an accounting period, all journal entries are summarized and transferred to the general ledger accounts. This procedure is called "posting."

3. **Making adjustments to the general ledger.**

General-ledger adjustments let businesses account for items that isn't recorded in daily journals, such as bad debts, and accrued interest or taxes. By adjusting entries, businesses can match revenues with expenses within each accounting period.

4. **Closing the books.**

A trial balance is prepared at the end of an accounting period by adding up all the account balances in your general ledger. The sum of the debit balances should equal the sum of the credit balances. If total debits don't equal total credits, you must track down the errors. After all revenues and expenses are accounted for, any net profit is posted in the equity account. Revenue and expense accounts are always brought to a zero balance before a new accounting cycle begins.

5. **Preparing financial statements.**

At the end of a period, businesses prepare financial reports - income statements, statements of capital, balance sheets, cash-flow statements and other reports - that summarize all of the financial activity for that period.

Your accounting records are important because the resulting financial statements and reports help you plan and make decisions. They may be used by some third parties (bankers, investors, or creditors) and may be needed to provide information to government agencies, such as the Internal Revenue Service.

Each year, J. Lyndon Johnson, president of Johnson Mortgage Services in Cincinnati, Ohio, reviews approximately $150 to $200 million in church loans. "With all of the churches I have helped with conventional loans or refinancing, one thing is common," he says. "Pastors are some of the worst financial managers I have ever dealt with. If I were to ask most pastors for church records, the chances are good they would hand me their checkbook."

That inadequacy usually affects how the church handles finances. Johnson says he receives calls from six to nine churches a day looking for financing, but few can provide reliable records. "In some cases, church bookkeeping hasn't changed in 40 years," he says.

One reason pastors lack financial acumen is that they were never educated in such matters. "Pastors are not trained to think financially," says Bob Welch, associate professor of administration at Southwestern Baptist Theological Seminary, in Fort Worth, Texas. Pastors aren't pleased with the inadequacy, however. According to Welch, the results of a recent poll among Southwestern alumni showed that 80 percent of the respondents expressed a desire to take church administration courses.[1]

DAY-TO-DAY TRANSACTIONS RECORDKEEPING

In order to take control of your financial recordkeeping, you must accurately record your day-to-day revenue, purchases, and other transactions. Specifically, you need to record:

- Revenue transactions (tithing, gifts, special events fees, etc.)
- Cash transactions (cash only purchases, gifts to those in need, etc.)
- Accounts receivable (pledges, payments from people for a retreat they attended, etc.)
- Accounts payable, (if you purchase from your suppliers on credit)

There are many computer programs on the market to help you automate your accounting procedures. Shop around. Accounting software is sold in office supply stores, software outlets, electronics stores, mail order houses, and directly from software publishers. Ask for your accountant's opinion. Your accountant may want you to use a program that is compatible with the system he or she uses.

If you have staff employees, look for accounting software that permits the use of passwords to control access to all or some of your accounting transactions. In order to prevent irregularities by your employees or others, it's wise to restrict access to your accounting records.

SUMMARY

Managing ministry resources is becoming more and more complicated. Operating a church in an organized and efficient manner is not as simple as it may have been a few decades ago. Many of the challenges that face a church include more government scrutiny, unethical practices by icons within the Christian community, an increased awareness by the members of a church and the general public regarding finances in light of secular mega companies' mismanagement.

Although the essential purpose of the church has not changed since the forming of the early church in the Book of Acts, financial accountability has changed significantly. The church cannot look to the government or secular corporations for the best fiscal practices. However, the one constant that has never changed is the fundamental principles, which have been laid out for us in scripture. Now more than ever, church ministries must turn to the scriptures to deal with the core of financial governance- integrity.

Integrity is at the core of everything we do, especially when dealing with the resources that the Lord provides. It is critical that we apply wisdom in all of our financial decisions, both personal and ministry related. We cannot practice one set of values in the secular world and then apply other standards in ministry. Both must be reconciled to the scriptures.

Managing God's resources begins at home. If we cannot manage the things that the Lord has given us in our homes, how can we expect to miraculously manage the Lord's resources in ministry? If we lower our standards of sound financial principles when we cross the threshold of our church, we cheat God and rob Him of the honor that is due Him.

Paul exhorts us in I Corinthians 14:40- "All things must be done properly and in an orderly manner." With this in mind, we must always bear witness of our relationship with Jesus Christ in our words and deeds. Our lives must be a living testimony to everyone around us as we conduct the business affairs of our Lord. To do anything less, will undermine and comprise our walk with Him. Even though God's church is not in business to make a profit, it's still the Lord's business! There is no substitute for responsible financial stewardship. We must apply ourselves at all times, because if we cannot be entrusted with Man's economy, how can we be entrusted with the Lord's "true riches"?

CHURCH ACCOUNTABILITY

To God: "It is required in stewards to be found faithful." I Corinthians 4:2

To Man: Because God has chosen to use people to supply the needs of the Church

To Government: Submission to all those placed in authority over us - Federal, State and Local government

References:

1. Michelsen, Jr., Michael W., "The Money-Wise Church", Your Church magazine, November/December, 2000.

PERSONAL APPLICATION

1. Identify three challenges of financial stewardship.

2. Describe why a ministry's Mission and Vision statements are essential to responsible financial stewardship.

3. What is the difference between Bookkeeping and Accounting?

4. Describe why some pastors make poor financial managers.

5. On a scale of 1 through 10 (1 being poor, 10 being expert), how would you rate your financial stewardship skills and why?

Ministry Organizational Development

The mind of a man plans his way, But the Lord directs his path
Proverbs 16:19

Organizations must continually changes in response to technological, social and economics; as well as to internal conditions from within the organization. By definition, organizational development is the ongoing planned process of change used as means of improving conditions and problem-solving capabilities to effectively cope with change.

Organizational development (OD) is the study of successful organizational change and performance. OD emerged from human relations studies in the 1930s, during which psychologists realized that organizational structures and processes influence worker behavior and motivation.

In short, planned change is synonymous with organizational development. Many leaders strongly believe that organizations should not wait for unwanted changes to be thrust on them. Instead, by anticipating and diagnosing these factors, they can plan more effective organizations[1].

Organization Development is an effort that is:

- Planned

- Organization-wide

- Managed from the top

- Increase organization effectiveness and health

CHARACTERISTICS OF CHANGE

In the past, organizational development professionals focused on implementing change, specifically human behavior. Structural processes are inanimate and without feeling, however the human factors that drive those processes are very much alive and directly effect change. Most often when change is necessary, it is not the structural processes that hinder changed, it is the resistance that comes from the feeling of those people who manage the structure.

In the early 1950"'s Kurt Lewin developed a technique for changing people's behaviors, skills and attitudes. He determined that there are two forces which effect an organization's behavior. One, those striving to maintain the status quo and; two, those pushing for change[2]. He also determined that in order to create change, you can increase the forces that are pushing for change and decrease the forces that are maintaining the current state, or some combination of the two. He contends that modifying the forces that are maintaining the status quo produces less tension and resistance than increasing forces of change.

Organizational development has three chief characteristics which address change-

- It reverses the process of change from traditional methods

- It identifies specific targets of change

- It involves a particular step-by-step process to advance change

Reversing traditional processes of change

The traditional change process assumed that management, accounting and other formal areas first decided what must be accomplished in a technical or structural sense.

Given this approach, the next step involved changing the actions of people to fit the strategy, one way or the other.

In contrast, today's organizational change approach starts with people first. Operating procedures, costs, job descriptions, production schedules, etc. have become dependent on how people feel about themselves and others, in relation to their work.

Identifying specific targets

The targets are certain attitudes, skill and behaviors of individual people. And who are these people? It is not exclusive to board of directions, top leadership or the people in the trenches. It can also include a group of people. Regardless of rank or status, they are a group of people who have studied the problem and are concerned about change.

Step-by-step targets

The third characteristic of organizational development involves a particular step sequence for the total change effort. The process runs the gamut from the vision or the plan to the solution of structural and technical problems.

The following steps provide a guide to planning for change:

1. Plan the change process

2. Change the attitudes and habits of individuals, specifically in the ways people treat others

3. Change group climate or culture (the collective attitudes and habits of individuals).

4. Work out new structures, such as:

   (a) New goals and objectives

   (b) Who is responsible for what (new personalized roles)

   (c) Who has the final authority over whom

GOING FORWARD RESPONSIBILITY

As the old say goes, "Aim for nothing, and you'll hit nothing". This is true in ministry as well in life. When leaders fail t plan or accommodate for chance, their ministries become like old wine skins. Wineskins, which if they are not used, inevitably become stiff, cracked and eventually burst. (Matthew (:14-17)

"If you don't know where you're going, any road will take you there."
~ George Harrison ~

At this point, some may raise the question if strategic planning is biblical? The answer is "Yes!" Planning within a ministry is not just something lifted from a secular business model. It is important to respond in the affirmative when asked if God honors the process of strategic planning. There are several biblical leaders who demonstrated strategic planning in their ministry.

Moses learned and applied strategic thinking as he led the nation of Israel through the wilderness. The human behaviors of the people were ever changing and becoming more dependent on Moses. Their dependency reached its peak when he was judging their issues almost all day and night. His father-in-law Jethro observed the strain and toll it was taking on Moses. In order to care for the people effectively, Jethro shared with him a God-given plan or strategy for dealing with the people and their issues. As a result, the manpower available was used more effectively and Moses was better for it.

Joshua, the disciple of Moses, demonstrated strategic leadership in the book of Joshua, chapter 6. As Joshua led the people into the Promised Land, they faced their first enemy in the strong city of Jericho. Rather than personally intervening, God was strategically creative in overcoming the enemy in Jericho through His people. God continues today to work through His people.

Nehemiah was called by God to rebuild the walls of Jerusalem. He began developing his strategic plan to change the conditions of the wall. Once he arrived in Jerusalem, he could have started laying the "structural" plans and forcing them on the people. But, instead, he strategically inspected the dilapidated wall and encouraged them to rebuild the wall by appealing to their pride as the children of God (Nehemiah 2:11-20)

Accomplishing God's purposes through strategic planning

Without question, it is God's plan that we want to accomplish, not our own. In order to begin the process, we must align our hearts with our Lord's. Proverbs 19:21 tells us that "Many are the plans in a man's heart, But the counsel of the Lord, it will stand." God's purpose is essential in our planning, which is can be drastically different from secular business models.

Our undergirding, should be, not to trust our plans and strategies, but rely on the Holy Spirit to guide us. Although we have ample biblical principles to guide us, they are faceless signposts if we are not in the will of God. We need to seek the heart of God first!

The scriptures are replete with strategic planning principles. The Proverbs alone speak volumes, for example; Proverbs 14: 15, 15:22, 16:3, 16:9 and 20:18.

Again, change is inevitable. Strategic planning allows leadership to set priorities that enables leaders to act confidently and responsibly. Leaders must make an intentional effort to seek the inspiration and guidance of the Holy Spirit. When they do, this discernment allows leaders to move into the future successfully and in God's plan.

MINIMIZING PITFALLS

To help steer you away from possible pitfalls, consider the following suggestions: Do not make the planning process too complex: Typically, there are only two or three key issues to address or change.

1. Do not make the planning process too complex: Typically, there are only two or three key issues to address or change.

2. Do not make an action plan before reaching conclusions: Ties up loose ends along the way and outline appropriate actions steps.

3. Do not make an action plan too complex: Keep the plan simple enough for anyone to follow.

4. Do not be afraid to revise the plan: The plan should be flexible, adjusted and revised along the way according to the needs and resources available to you.

5. Do not take too long to plan: Do not let the planning team tire of the process and complain about the value of the plan.

6. Trust God's empowering presence through the planning process: Trust in God's leading through His Holy Spirit

ORGANIZATIONAL DEVELOPMENT BASED ON BIBLICAL PRINCIPLES: 7 TIPS FOR FORMING A TOP-NOTCH ENTERPRISE

In an article written and titled "Organizational Development Based on Biblical Principles: 7 Tips for Forming a Top-notch Enterprises[4]" posted by Eric Coggins on January 6, 2009 on the website www.ezinarticles.com, he shares 7 valuable tips help to align organizational development with biblical principles.

Eric Coggins writes:

Lessons for sound organizational development can be found in many ways and from many sources. One of the most referenced sources has been the Bible. A simple read of the first four chapter of Genesis will show the learning leader why the Bible is such a gold mine of development principles and is applicable even to those mangers or leaders who do not espouse a belief in God. This article discusses seven relevant tis for forming a well-developed enterprise found in the opening chapters of Genesis.

Tip One: Effective Organizational Leaders Create an Empowering Atmosphere

First, from Genesis chapters one and two, the corporate director (ministry leader) can learn: the leader or management team sets the tone and atmosphere for the organization. He/She designs and orchestrates each aspect of the enterprise in such a way that all parts and participants can thrive at their optimum level. This principle is seen in the account of how God designed and created the universe and the earth.

Tip Two: The Best Enterprise (Ministry) Developers Recruit and Release Others to Help Fulfill the Corporate (Ministry) Vision

In the same two chapters, the organizational developer realizes: the leader or management team employs others in the work of the organization. The enterprise will not grow to its fullest potential as a one man show. A leader recruits others to work alongside and releases them to do their part.

Tip Three: Value-Added Organizational Design Includes Well-Defined Job Descriptions and Rules of Order

Furthermore, from chapter two of Genesis, it can be ascertained that the top-notch leader or management team writes job descriptions and sets down rules of authority and engagement. God created the first man, gave him the job of taking care of his surroundings, and set only one rule to establish proper lines of authority.

Tip Four: Effective Motivators Initiate Relationships in the Best and Worst of Times

In Genesis chapters two, three and four; it can be observed that God not only set the organization in motion, but was also heavily involved in the day to day lives of the people. By initiating and maintaining solid relationships with Adam, Eve and their children, God knew them and identified their needs even before they expressed them. After Adam and Eve violated the company rules, God did not simply turn his back on them, but sought them out. He remained concerned about their welfare even though they had failed miserably.

Tip Five: Successful Organizational Developers Confront Bad Behavior and Discipline Gross Violations

Chapters three and four of Genesis record God's confrontation with Adam and Eve (chapter three) and their son Cain (chapter four). In each case they had failed to carry out the corporate policies of the organization. Adam and Eve ate of the forbidden tree while Cain brought an unacceptable gift to God. In the case of Cain, God gave him an opportunity to recognize his weakness and follow a new course of action. When Cain chose to follow his own painful road, God cut him loose.

Tip Six: Empowering Managers Recognize Excellent Performance

This principle is seen in God's approval of Abel's offering. Abel offered his best and God was quick to acknowledge and accept that offering. The best corporate (ministry) leaders learn to do the same. They are involved with their employees (staff and volunteers) and appreciate the efforts they give. When they see superior performance the most successful bosses acknowledge that performance and even reward them with an extra bonus or some other type of worthwhile compensation.

Tip Seven: The Best Corporate (Ministry) Developers Offer Hope and Create New Opportunities Out of Failure

When Adam and Eve broke the only company rule, they disqualified themselves from fulfilling God's original design. So God, being the most imaginative organizational developer of all, created a new opportunity that offered hope for a positive future.

Lessons for sound organizational development can be found from many sources. One of the most referenced sources has been the Bible. A simple read of the first four chapters of Genesis will show the learning leader why the Bible is such a gold mine of development principles and is applicable even to those managers or leaders who do not espouse a belief in God. This article has discussed seven relevant tips for forming a well-developed enterprise.

Eric Coggins has a BA in Political Science and an MBA in Global Management. He has lived and worked abroad and has had interaction with members of many different ethnic backgrounds including African, American, Latin American, Japanese, Korean, Cambodian, Australian and European.

References

1. Hitt, Michael A.; Middlesmist, R., Dennis; Mathis, Robert L.; "Management Concepts and Effective Practice", West Publishing Company, St. Paul, Minnesota, 1983, page 384.

2. Lussier, Robert N., "Management Concepts, Applications, Skill Development", South-Western College Publishing, Cincinnati, Ohio, 1997, page 263.

3. Macchia, Stephen, A., "Developing a Strategic Plan for Your Church", Christianity Today, (online article), www.christianitytodaay.com/bcl/areas/vision-strategy/articles/070204.html, July 2, 2004.

4. Cogging, Eric, "Organizational Development Based on Biblical Principles: 7 Tips for Forming a Top-notch Enterprises⁹", posted January 6, 2009, website www.ezinarticles.com.

5. Victor P. K. Mensah, "Church Management", posted January 8, 2010, website http://wikieducator.org/Church_management/Introduction

SUMMARY

Organizations must continually change in response to technological, social and economic forces, as well as internal forces emerging from the organization itself. In order to avoid stagnating, church or ministry leadership must keep a keen eye on possible changes on the horizon. The watchman cannot be caught sleeping on the wall. Vigilance is essential in keeping ahead of change and adjusting to it.

Although many forces exert pressure for a change in an organization, change is often resisted because it possesses a threat to those most effected by change. This real or perceived threat can adversely drive behaviors, which can hinder, or halt needed change. Leaders must anticipate resistance to change and develop strategies to minimize its impact.

Ministry organizational development refers to long-range efforts to improve an organization's problem-solving capabilities and the ability to cope with necessary changes. Leaders must remember to address the issues and concerns of the human element of change before focusing on structural change. Reversing the process may lead to a prolonged or failed outcome.

One objective is clear. Strategic planners within a church or ministry must understand-know who you are as a church or ministry. Consider the following before you begin any organizational development process-

The Three Most Important Things Every Church Should Know About Itself [5]

Why does our church or ministry exist?

A multitude of churches and ministries exist for a multitude of reasons. Some are church plants (or much needed ministries) put in place to round out a denomination's geographic coverage. Others spring up independently to fill a perceived spiritual gap in the community. Other congregations are the by-product of a church split or theological split within their denomination or organization.

So why does your church/ministry exist? If it's for the Great Commission, how faithfully are you pursuing it? If it's to build god-fearing families, how are marriages and kids holding up? If your church/ministry is keen on community outreach, what impact are you making at the grassroots level? If you're a disciple-making congregation (or purpose driven ministry), how many spiritually reproducing disciples are hard at Kingdom work? If you exist for social activism, has your community benefited from greater justice, equality, and sharing of wealth? Are you a holiness church/ministry relying on God's mighty Spirit to miraculously transform and renew lives? If so, is the agape love of members/staff/volunteers for one another maturing and deepening? Have their lives been transported to a higher spiritual plain?

Does your congregation/ministry have a declared mission? What difference is your church/ministry making in the lives of other people? What will your legacy be?

How does our church fit into God's plans?

What makes your church/ministry special, reflecting God's special work in your midst? Has he blessed you with ministries few other congregations/organizations offer? Do you have certain "magnet" ministries that pull in a steady stream of new members/staff/volunteers/donors? Is your church/ministry overflowing with baptisms/meeting needs? Are you reaching a unique group or subculture of people (the homeless, the incarcerated, unwed mothers, families in crisis, at-risk teens, etc.) overlooked or ignored by other churches or ministries? Do you have a discipleship or missions program that regularly sends new missions workers into the spiritual harvest fields of the world? Are you a sacrificing, giving congregation/ministry? Are you a multiple generation family church/ministry of "rock of ages" members with deep roots in that one congregation? Does Christ shine in and through your members/staff/volunteers?

What brings people to our church or ministry?

Is it your great facilities, vibrant mid-week family programs, or your minister's sermons, your purpose for fulfilling a need? Are visitors attracted by the spiritual maturity of your members, or maybe by the congregation's diversity in age, ethnicity, or socioeconomic status? Are volunteers and donors draw to your ministry because of the visible passion of what you do? Do you know what your church or ministry is doing "right" to attract new members, staff, donors, and volunteers?

PERSONAL APPLICATION

1. Identify one or two impending changes in your church, ministry or work environment

2. Describe what steps can be implemented to accommodate the necessary changes. Remember to address the human concerns before any structural changes are recommended.

3. Describe the benefits of the changes.

Vision and Mission Development

Vison: ^{2} Then the Lord answered me and said, "Record the vision And inscribe it on tablets, That the one who reads it may run. ^{3} "For the vision is yet for the appointed time; It hastens toward the goal and it will not fail. Though it tarries, wait for it; For it will certainly come, it will not delay. Habakkuk 2:2-3

Mission: "^{18} And Jesus came up and spoke to them, saying, "All authority has been given to Me in heaven and on earth. ^{19} Go therefore and make disciples of all the nations, baptizing them in the name of the Father and the Son and the Holy Spirit, ^{20} teaching them to observe all that I commanded you; and lo, I am with you always, even to the end of the age."
Matthew 28:18-20

Much has been said, written and taught about developing organizational or personal "Vision", "Mission" and "Core Values" statements. There are myriads of information on the-who, what, why, when and where of developing these three statements. The two main questions that beg to be answered- one, "Why are these statements needed?" and; two, "How are they developed? Those two questions alone open up another multitude of questions. The good news is that the concept is biblical and they provide focus to any organization that seeks the Lord's will in whatever an organization has been called to do for the Kingdom.

An organization or church can adopt simple Vison and Mission statements such as in the following examples below-

Vision: "That all would know Jesus and His Saving Grace."

Mission: "To encourage all to live their Life's Journey one day at a time, serving the Lord as they pursue His purpose for their life."

Core Values: "Caring for others- we regularly fund charities and local community groups from the profits of our business"

Or, a more comprehensive approach can be utilized through a process and series of steps to develop an in-depth profile of an organization. There is no right or wrong approach. What matters is that an organization accomplishes two things- identity and purpose. Everything else, is the color commentating for the story.

This module will follow a simple outline in developing the various statements. However, the content within the various components of the outline will be complete and enable you the reader to use this module as a road map. This road map will also leave room for customization for your unique ministry or church.

Before you begin the core of this module, the first important aspect of this module is to identify the expected "learning outcomes". The points below speak to what you should accomplish in your understanding of all the material you will review and learn.

Expected Learning Outcomes

- Develop an understanding of a Vision, Mission and Core Values statement
- Understanding what is the difference between these statements?
- Understand how to craft each statement

Mission, Vision and Core Values Statements Outline

I.   What is a Vison statement?

II.   What is Mission statement?

III.   What is the purpose or importance of a Vision, Mission and Core Values statement?

IV.   Understanding the difference between a Vision, Mission and Core Vales statement

V.   How to develop a Vison and Mission statement

WHAT IS A VISION STATEMENT?

Vision is a concept that refers to someone's mental image or revelation of the future. It refers to the ideal future concept of conditions that someone can imagine for one's self or an organization.

A vision is an outline of a desired outcome to be acquired within a specified period of time. Although the vision is a desired end, nevertheless, it's expected to be achievable because it's based on a sound understanding of the current conditions and a realistic assessment of those conditions.

Your vision is your dream. It's what your organization believes are the ideal conditions for your purpose, community or calling; that is, how things would look if the issue important to you were completely, perfectly addressed. It might be a world full of Christian believers, or a world without poverty and homelessness, or a community in which all people are treated as equals, regardless of gender or racial background.

Whatever your organization's dream is, it may be well articulated by one or more *vision statements*. Vision statements are short phrases or sentences that convey your organization or ministry hopes for the future. By developing a vision statement or statements, your organization clarifies the beliefs and governing principles of your organization or ministry, first for your calling, and then for the greater purpose of that calling.

Simply put, a Vison statement is a brief one or two sentence statement describing the clear and inspirational ling-term change, resulting from your work.

A Vision Statement Needs To . . .

- ☐ . . . clear and simple (many are not)
- ☐ . . . avoid elaborate language and buzz words
- ☐ . . . easily explained by those involved
- ☐ . . . not to be confused by a Mission statement

Questions To Answer

- ☐ What needs to be changed?
  - ○ What are the major issues or problems?
- ☐ What are the strengths and resources available?
  - ○ For the organization/ministry and those being served
- ☐ What does your dream look like at the end?
  - ○ In a perfect world, what would the vision look like?
- ☐ What does the vision look like if it's successfully accomplished?
  - ○ Be specific in stating the final outcome

Lastly, by developing a vision statement or statements, your organization clarifies the beliefs and governing principles of your organization, first for yourselves, and then for the greater audience.

There are certain characteristics that most vision statements have in common. In general, vision statements should be:

- Understood and shared by the people you serve
- Specific enough to attract people who share similar perspectives
- Inspiring and uplifting to everyone involved in your effort
- Easy to communicate - for example, they are generally short enough to fit on a T-shirt

WHAT IS A MISSION STATEMENT?

The Mission statement can be as short as a one sentence statement to a short paragraph describing the reason an organization, program or ministry exists. Mission statements come in all shapes and sizes from the short to the lengthy, from the vague to the detailed or quantifiable. Ultimately, it comes down to what statement is right for your organization or ministry. Typically, it is normally short, to the point and contains the following elements-

- Provides a concise statement of why the organization exists, and what it will achieve

- States the purpose an identity of the organization, ministry or program

- Defines the organization, ministry or program's values and philosophy

- Describes how the organization, ministry or program will serve those affected by its work

It's worthy to note that there are some common characteristics among meaningful mission statements. Those characteristics include-

- <u>Make the statement as concise as possible</u>: Preferably concise enough to promote a 30 second infomercial

- <u>Make it memorable</u>: Preferably what is stated is something that people will remember, especially the key points of the statement

- <u>Make it distinctive</u>: Preferably stating something that doesn't sound "cookie cutter" or cut and pasted from other statements. Focus on how your organization or ministry is different

- <u>Make it realistic</u>: Preferably it does not sound like a vision statement. The statement is a description of the present, not the future

- <u>Make it current</u>: Preferably is not set in stone. The statement should be pliable and able to be revised when your focus changes

Unlike the Vision statement (a statement focusing on the future) the Mission statement focuses on the current work of the organization. The Mission statement outlines- "who we are", "what we do" and "for whom do we do it for". The statement also provides a concise summary of the organization, ministry or program's purpose. The Mission statement also answers "why" the organization, ministry or program exists.

To be effective, a Mission statement not only addresses the "who we are" and "who we want to be" of an organization or ministry, it should also be designed to inspire commitment from staff and loyalty from volunteers and anyone else who desires to contribute to the organization or ministry. And yes, you will want to get input from every insider and outsider involved with your organization or ministry.

What it does is convey in <u>concise</u> terms, in easy-to- understand everyday language, how an organization or ministry defines itself: its values, attitude towards the community it serves, vision, and a measure of success. Guiding principles elaborate on that statement, providing added specific information on how that mind-set applies to day-to-day business. Your MO or modus operandi so to speak.

Keeping both the statement and principles simple and straightforward is no small undertaking. You want the mission statement to be short and sweet, to the point, and easy enough for everyone to remember. You will be forced to strip away any "spin" from your thinking and focus, focus, focus!

WHAT IS THE IMPORTANCE OF A VISION, MISSION AND CORE VALUES STATEMENT?

The importance of having a vision, mission and core value statements is often underestimated. They are succinct declarations of your purpose, ideal future and what you believe. They serve as the lighthouse for the organization and its supports to align everyone on the path and the destination.

Statements are standard and critical elements of organizational strategy. Most established organizations and ministries develop organizational vision, mission and core value statements, which serve as foundational guides in the establishment of organizational objectives. The organization or ministry then develops strategic and tactical plans for objectives.

DIFFERENCE BETWEEN MISSION AND VISION

The mission statement is a statement of purpose, and a vision is a statement of where one is going.

Organizations summarize their goals and objectives in mission and vision statements. Both of these serve different purposes for an organization, but are often confused with each other. While a mission statement describes what an organization wants to do *now*, a vision statement outlines what an organization wants to be in the *future*.

The Mission Statement concentrates on the present; it defines the target recipients, critical processes and it informs the organization about the desired level of performance.

The Vision Statement focuses on the future; it is a source of inspiration and motivation. Often it describes not just the future of the organization but the future of the industry or society in which the organization hopes to effect change.

Which comes first?

Vision, mission or core values statement? To quote Dorothy from the film The Wizard of Oz- "It's always best to start at the beginning . . . ." An organization's core values are the heart and soul of its purpose and vision. Without knowing what you believe, its fruitless to develop mission (the "what") or the vison (the "when") statements. First things first, "what do you believe?"

Then, successively, for a new start up organization, ministry, new program or plan to re-engineer your current purpose, the vision statement will be formulated next as it will guide the mission statement and the rest of the strategic plan.

For an established organization or ministry where the mission is established, often the mission guides the vision statement and the rest of the strategic plan for the future.

Comparison Chart

Mission Statement vs. Vision Statements		
	Mission Statement	**Vision Statement**
About	A Mission statement talks about HOW you will get to where you want to be. Defines the purpose and primary objectives related to your customer needs and team values.	A Vision statement outlines WHERE you want to be. Communicates both the purpose and values of your business.
Answer	It answers the question, "What do we do? What makes us different?"	It answers the question, "Where do we aim to be?"
Time	A mission statement talks about the present leading to its future.	A vision statement talks about your future.
Function	It lists the broad goals for which the organization is formed. Its prime function is internal; to define the key measure or measures of the organization's success and its prime audience is the leadership, team and stockholders.	It lists where you see yourself some years from now. It inspires you to give your best. It shapes your understanding of why you are working here.
Change	Your mission statement may change, but it should still tie back to your core values, customer needs and vision.	As your organization evolves, you might feel tempted to change your vision. However, mission or vision statements explain your organization's foundation, so change should be kept to a minimum.
Developing a statement	What do we do today? For whom do we do it? What is the benefit? In other words, Why we do what we do? What, For Whom and Why?	Where do we want to be going forward? When do we want to reach that stage? How do we want to do it?
Features of an effective statement	Purpose and values of the organization: Who are the organization's primary "clients" (stakeholders)? What are the responsibilities of the organization towards the clients?	Clarity and lack of ambiguity: Describing a bright future (hope); Memorable and engaging expression; realistic aspirations, achievable; alignment with organizational values and culture.

1. Ministry Goals: What goals are the Holy Spirit leading us to strive for to enhance (or change) our church or ministry over the next year? The next two to three years?

2. Action Steps: What action steps must we accomplish to achieve these goals (or changes)?

The key to fulfilling the task of answering the questions will be to gain a consensus from the leadership team. Even if everyone involved in the planning process is under the submission of the Holy Spirit, it may or may not be difficult depending on the all the factors involved.

WHAT IS A CORE VALUES STATEMENT?

Definition: A principle that guides an organization's internal conduct as well as its relationship with the external world. Core values are usually summarized in the mission statement or in a statement of core values.

Core values are traits or qualities that you consider not just worthwhile, they represent an individual's or an organization's highest priorities, deeply held beliefs, and core, fundamental driving forces. They are the heart of what your organization and its employees stand for in the world.

Core values define what your organization believes and how you want your organization resonating (or echoing) with and appealing to employees (staff) and the external world.

The core values should be so integrated with your employees (staff) and their belief systems and actions that clients, customers, and vendors see the values in action.

For example, the heart and core value of successful small to mid-sized companies is evident in how they serve customers. When customers tell the company or organization that they feel cherished by the business, you know that your employees (staff) are living your core value of extraordinary customer care and service.

Core values are also known as guiding principles because they form a solid core of who you are, what you believe, and who you are and want to be going forward.[1]

So, if mission statements tell the reader what your organization currently expects to achieve and the vision statement articulates where an organization expects to be, then the purpose of stating your core values is to help define the type of organization you strive to be. It describes your culture, your ethics and your priorities. Your stated values represent the "how" along with the "what" and "where" of your mission and vision statement.

It's good to note that all these high-level statements are only of value if the words are transformed into actions or deeds. For example, a new car may look great in the inside and the all the promotional advertising may speak of its future potential, but what really counts is what you find under the hood!

Core values can help to remind the organization of what is important and to make sure that these qualities don't go by the wayside. This is especially essential when day-to-day activities consume the day or pursuing the vision overshadows those important values. In order for the core values of any organization to be practical it's critical that your defined values are specific and meaningful. A cookie-cutter list of just words and phrases that may sound appealing will not mask the genuine core beliefs and practices of an organization.

Defining an organization's values should be creative and collaborative. Who and how to involve people can provide a wider perspective and encourage buy-in. Sensitivities will surface throughout the development process. All the efforts to define the organization'ss values will eventually touch on issues and personal points of view.

Views, opinions and biases like personal ethics, morals and beliefs will come into play during the development process. The final values may reflect the diversity of all everyone involved in the development process, however, because it's a shared process, the final values should also reflect at the very least an agreed consensus of those involved. As a word of caution, if tact and diplomacy are not handled properly, the potential for unwanted tensions and alienation can surface.

For every value that is identified, they should point to every nook and cranny of the organization. There should be no effort to find all the agreed upon values saturating not only the organization, but the all the people associated with them by demonstrating values in action. Simply put- "If you talk the talk, then, walk the walk".

Although there is no limit to the amount of stated core values, it is important only state those values reflect your organization's traits and priorities. Experientially, the average amount of values is six. Ten stated values is typically the maximum and three being the minimum. What matters the most is that you have encapsulated the heart of what it is that makes your organization who you are.

Ultimately an organization must live the developed and stated values as its genuine DNA. Organizations must resist the temptation to treat the core values as a finished product. It's good to remember that the stated values are living and breathing statements with the flexibility to expand or contract and needed.

Bottom-line, in order for an organization to be effective, it's values must be something agreed upon, shared and genuinely believed by everyone in the organization. Otherwise, the values have no genuine meaning, and they become just another corporate impersonal slogan, words on a website and a worthless refection of who the organization is. In other words, a body without a soul and heart.

Downside to Identifying Values

The downside to identifying values occurs when an organization's leadership claim certain values and then behave in ways that are contradictory to their stated values. In these environments, values devalue motivation because employees or staff don't trust their leaders' word.

Remember that employees or staff are like radar machines watching everything you as a leader do, listening to everything you say, and watching your interaction with stakeholders, customers and even their coworkers. They see your values in action every day at work—or not. Never underestimate the power of values in creating a motivating work environment—or not

THE STATEMENT DEVELOPMENT PROCESS

Before getting entangled in the details of the precise wording and phrasing, the most important task is to successfully identify the major elements of your organization or ministry. Think through how these elements will define and communicate your organization's purpose, expected future and what you believe. These elements represent the core of what you feel represent the best of your organization and what is endeavor to achieve.

As you begin the process, ask the following questions-

- Who will be involved in development process?

- Who are we and why do we exist?

- Where are we going and why?

- What information do we need to make our strategic decisions?

- What are the strategic topics and issues we need to address through this process?

- What is already determined that we need to build off?

Specific elements to the statement process-

Vision

Your vision should:

- describe the ideal future you want for your users or cause

- capture the heart and the head, and have an idealistic tone

- convey a standard of excellence

- reflect horizon-expanding ideals

- inspire enthusiasm and commitment
- use language that's easily understood
- link with your mission
- show that change is needed

Mission

Your mission statement should say:

- Who you are
- Who or what you support
- What you do
- Why you do it
- How you do it.

It should be:

- Clear and easily understood
- Short and focused (usually one or two sentences)
- Inspiring
- Realistic, workable and achievable
- Expressed in terms of outcomes
- Linked to your charitable objectives (if it isn't, then these should be reviewed too – but remember that amending your objects is a major step)
- Remember that amending your objects is a major step

Core Values

Values are:

- Things that people feel have value or worth and hold dear
- Beliefs, attitudes or principles expressed in behaviors
- Things that govern organizational behavior – what people do and how they do it
- Consistent with each other and with your vision and mission.

Statement Construction Methodology[2]

Rather than starting with an unstructured brainstorming session, it may help to take a step back and start with utilizing simple "building blocks" and frameworks.

There are two approaches that can be utilized to develop a vision, mission or values statement- "Simple Approach" or "Comprehensive Approach". Either method will work depending on your perspective, need and resources.

I. The **Simple Approach** is straight forward and only involves pairing or combining "high priority" actions with "whom you wish to target".

Example: **Action + Target Receiver**

"**Protect** all *unborn children* in every community."

Action		Target Receiver

"**To serve** *families in the poorest communities in the county*"

Action		Target Receiver

"**Raise** the *awareness* of homelessness in the city"

Action	Target Receiver

"**Nourishing** *the Flock* Through God's Word"

Action	Target Receiver

II. The **Comprehensive Approach** encompasses not only actions and target receivers, but includes other components in building a statement. Other components can include- **service(s), problem(s), partner(s) and cause(s).**

To keep your message clear and uncluttered, apply no more that 4 to 5 components. Also, limit your word connector to one if possible, e.g., "inspire *and* inspire" or "homelessness, hunger *and* social responsibility".

Examples:

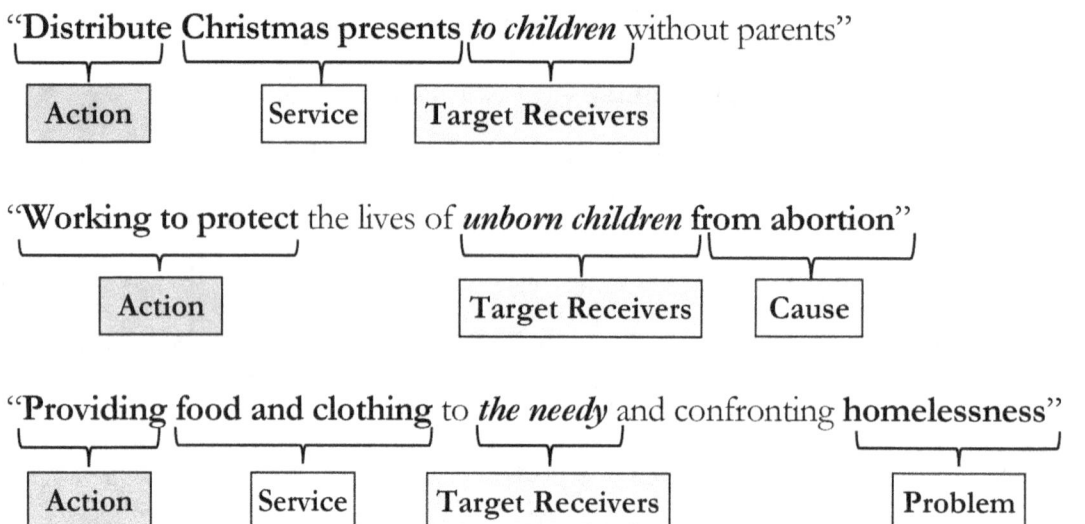

EXAMPLES OF VISON STATEMENTS

- **Make-A-Wish**: That people everywhere will share the power of a wish (10 words)

- **Alzheimer's Association**: A world without Alzheimer's (4 words)

- **Feeding America**: A hunger-free America (4 words)

- **Habitat for Humanity**: A world where everyone has a decent place to live. (10 words)

- **San Diego Zoo**: To become a world leader at connecting people to wildlife and conservation. (12 words)

EXAMPLES OF MISSION STATEMENTS

- **3M:** To solve unsolved problems innovatively.

- **International Red Cross:** To provide relief to victims of disaster and help people prevent, prepare for, and respond to emergencies.

- **Boy Scouts of America:** To preserve the values and benefits of wilderness for present and future generations by connecting agency employees and the public with their wilderness heritage through training, information, and education.

- **Starbucks:** To inspire and nurture the human spirit — one person, one cup and one neighborhood at a time.

- **The Elephant Sanctuary:** A natural-habitat refuge where sick, old, and needy elephants can once again walk the earth in peace and dignity.

- **Fannie Mae:** To provide liquidity, stability and affordability to the U.S. housing and mortgage markets.

- **Google:** To organize the world's information and make it universally accessible and useful.

- **Walmart:** We save people money so they can live better.

- **Marine Stewardship Council:** To safeguard the world's seafood supply by promoting the best environmental choices.

- **Marriott Hotels:** To make people who are away from home feel they are among friends and really wanted.

- **Merck:** To operate a worldwide business that produces meaningful benefits for consumers, our market partners and our community.

EXAMPLES OF CORE VALUES

- **Integrity:** We do what is right even when no one is watching.

- **Excellence:** We are constantly redefining our goals, expectations, boundaries, and potential.

- **Community Impact:** We use our talents and treasures to make a difference in those who need it most.

- **Spiritual Growth:** We provide the opportunity for all to know God and make Him known.

AFTER THE STATEMENTS ARE DEVELOPED, WHAT NEXT?

Once you've developed the vision, mission and core values statements then upcoming changes are identified. Conceptually, the process is not as daunting as one might perceive. Developing a strategic plan can be accomplished by answering *seven key questions.*[3]

1. Spiritual need assessment: What are the greatest spiritual needs of our church, ministry or community?

2. Strengths and weaknesses: What are the greatest strengths and weaknesses of the church or ministry?

3. Opportunities and threats or barriers (especially as it applies to change). What are the most significant ministry opportunities for potential threats (or barriers) to our church or ministry, given the answers t the first two questions?

4. Ministry Options: What appear to be the most viable options for strengthening (or changing) our church or ministry?

5. Ministry Platform (foundation): What is the primary ministry platform (foundation) on which our specific ministry should be built on? Included in the ministry platform (foundation) are- your statement of faith, vision statement, mission statement, philosophy of ministry, etc.

6. Ministry Goals: What goals is the Holy Spirit leading us to strive for to enhance (or change) our church or ministry over the next year? The next two to three years?

7. Action Steps: What action steps must we accomplish to achieve these goals (or changes)?

The key to fulfilling the task of answering the questions will be gaining a consensus from the leadership team. Even if everyone involved in the planning process is under the submission of the Holy Spirit, it may or may not be difficult depending on the circumstances and relationships of the leader involved.

References

1. Heathfield, Susan M., "Core Values Are What You Believe", posted September 27, 2017, website www.thebalance.com

2. "Mission Building Blocks", posted January 2017, website www.topnonprofits.com

3. Evans, Jennel, "Vision and Mission: Unleashing the power of vision and mission", posted April 24, 2010, www.psychologytoday.com/blog/smartwork/201004/vision-and-mission

SUMMARY

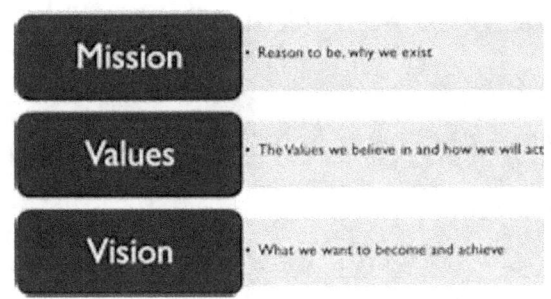

In the opinion of Jennell Evans of Smart@Work[3], not having a clearly defined Vision and Mission statements limits opportunities for the organization's success, and is a disservice to employees or staff who show up for work every day. If an organization wants engaged and productive employees/staff, it should make sure that they know how their work contributes to accomplishing the Mission (current state) and ultimately to the Vision (future state).

In addition to other benefits already mentioned, clear Vision, Mission and Core Values statements can:

- Strengthen culture through a unified sense of purpose
- Improve decision-making with clarity about "big picture"
- Enhance cross-functional relationships through a shared understanding of priorities

It's never too late for an organization to define its Vision, Mission and Core Values. Some even reinvent themselves through the strategic planning process, beginning with these three core elements.

Different approaches for developing a Vision, Mission and Core Values statements range from online tools for self-directed work groups, to engaging a professional strategic planner to facilitate the group discussions and manage the development process over a period of several months.

Regardless of how an organization creates an effective Vision, Mission and Core Values statement, it is important that they be embedded into the culture through clear and consistent communications from the highest levels of an organization.

As Jack Welch, Chairman, General Electric said, "Good business leaders create a vision, articulate the vision, passionately own the vision, and relentlessly drive it to completion."

What about you and your organization? Do you know what your organization's Vision, Mission and Core Values statements are? Can you articulate them? If so, how have they impacted the culture?

PERSONAL APPLICATION

Develop a Vision and Mission statement utilizing the building blocks technique to formulate your statement. You can work with two different types of building blocks methods;

1. Simple Approach: The most straightforward approach to combine a high-level action with a targeted beneficiary.

   ### Action + Targeted Audience

   Examples:

   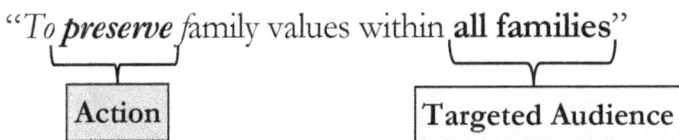

   *"To **preserve** family values within **all families**"*

   *"Care **for veterans** through no-cost services centers"*

   *"To minister to the **poorest population** in our city"*

2. **More Comprehensive Approaches:**

   Action(s) + Service(s) + Targeted Audience

   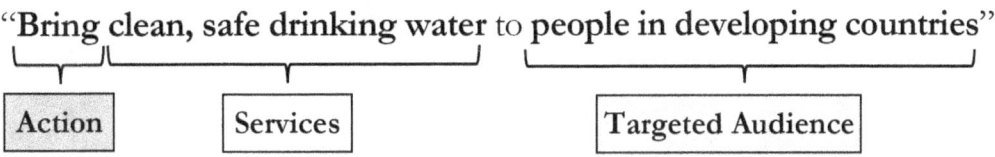

   "Bring clean, safe drinking water to people in developing countries"

Use the **ONE-PAGE VISION AND MISSION WORKSHEETS** (by Top Nonprofits website, copyright 2017) in the subsequent pages to create your statements.

Guidelines for selecting and completing each building block

- ❏ Choose 2-4 building blocks. 5 maximum
- ❏ 1 word string (A, B, & C). Choose wisely
- ❏ Target less than 20 syllables total. 30 maximum
- ❏ 5-14 words total. 20 maximum
- ❏ 8th to 10th grade reading level
- ❏ Avoid long or complicated words

ONE-PAGE VISION WORKSHEET

by  TopNonprofits

VISION STATEMENT DEFINITION

> A short phrase describing the future you are ultimately working towards (i.e. your final destination or desired end state)

HOW A VISION STATEMENT DIFFERS FROM A MISSION STATEMENT.

Mission statements and vision statements are complementary but unique.

MISSION
- Present tense
- Describes what you do and who/what benefits from this work

VISION
- Future Objective
- Description of a future you are ultimately working towards

Example from

MISSION: *To create lasting solutions to poverty, hunger, and social injustice.*

VISION: *A just world without poverty.*

GUIDELINES YOUR VISION STATEMENT SHOULD FOLLOW

Clear (Easy to Understand)
- ☐ Simple and concrete language
- ☐ 8th grade reading level. 10th max
- ☐ Avoid buzzwords and jargon

Concise (Sort & To the Point)
- ☐ 5-14 words (20 max)
- ☐ Avoid words > 12 letters or 4 syllables
- ☐ No more than 1 word string (A, B, and C)

BRAINSTORMING QUESTIONS

What would the world look like if this problem was solved?

If you were completely successful, what would this look like for you and your customers?

(Rare) Do you want to self impose a timeline? (Good for urgency. Awkward if not achieved.)

ONE-PAGE MISSION WORKSHEET   by

Guidelines for selecting and completing each building block

- Choose 2-4 building blocks. 5 max.
- 5-14 words total. 20 max.
- 1 word string (A, B, & C). Choose wisely.

- 8th grade reading level. 10th grade max.
- Target < 20 syllables total. 30 max.
- Avoid long or complicated words

ACTION(S)   High level action verb(s) to kick things off. "To_____ ..."

List options. Circle your top 1 or 2.

TARGETED BENEFICIARIES   The who/what that benefits from your work the most.

Super-Short Version (1-3 words)

Somewhat Short Version (4-8 words)

SERVICE(S)   What service(s) do you provide?

PROBLEM(S)   What problems does your products or services solve?

CAUSE   Is there an overarching cause you support?

PARTNERS   Are there any non-standard partners that are critical to your model?

* Indicates strongly recommended. All others optional.

Now on a separate piece of paper or whiteboard, string selected blocks into a draft mission statement. Continue refining and compressing until the result fits within guidelines.

© Copyright TopNonprofits, 2017.   Need help or have questions? Email: craig@topnonprofits.com